FIREWATER

HOW ALCOHOL IS KILLING MY PEOPLE (AND YOURS)

HAROLD R. JOHNSON

University of Regina Press

COVER AND TEXT DESIGN: Duncan Campbell, University of Regina Press
COPY EDITOR: Patricia Sanders
PROOFREADER: Kristine Douaud
INDEXER: Patricia Furdek
COVER ART: "Portrait of Harold Johnson," by Hamilton Photographics
TABLE OF CONTENTS AND SECTION PAGE ART: Treaty 6 with Saskatchewan Cree, 1876. *Glenbow Archives NA-1315-19*

Library and Archives Canada Cataloguing in Publication
Johnson, Harold, 1957-, author
    Firewater: how alcohol is killing my people (and yours)
/ Harold R. Johnson.

Includes bibliographical references.
Issued in print and electronic formats.
ISBN 978-0-88977-437-7 (paperback).—ISBN 978-0-88977-438-4
(pdf).—ISBN 978-0-88977-439-1 (html)

1. Indians of North America—Alcohol use—Canada.
2. Alcoholism—Social aspects—Canada. 3. Alcoholism—Treatment—Canada.
4. Drinking of alcoholic beverages—Social aspects—Canada.
5. Drinking of alcoholic beverages—History. 6. Spiritual healing.
I. Title.

E78.C2J625 2016   62.292'08997071   C2016-904746-6
                                                  C2016-904747-4

10   9   8   7   6   5   4   3

University of Regina Press, University of Regina
Regina, Saskatchewan, Canada, S4S 0A2
TEL: (306) 585-4758 FAX: (306) 585-4699
WEB: www.uofrpress.ca
U OF R PRESS   EMAIL: uofrpress@uregina.ca

We acknowledge the support of the Canada Council for the Arts for our publishing program. We acknowledge the financial support of the Government of Canada. / Nous reconnaissons l'appui financier du gouvernement du Canada. This publication was made possible through Creative Saskatchewan's Creative Industries Production Grant Program.

 Canada Council   Conseil des Arts   Canadä   creative
for the Arts   du Canada   SASKATCHEWAN

CONTENTS

PART 3—LETTERS FROM OUR SCOUTS, THE ARTISTS

PART 4—*NIYÂK*: FOR THE FUTURE

Treaty 6 territory in Saskatchewan.

PREFACE: THE AUTHOR'S FIRST WORDS TO HIS READERS

This small book is a conversation between myself and my relatives, the Woodland Cree. Its purpose is to begin a discussion about the harmful impacts of alcohol consumption and to address the extreme death rate directly connected to the use of alcohol in our northern Saskatchewan communities.

Some of what I am about to say may sound harsh when the discussion turns to the things that are being said about us. You may not want to hear those phrases repeated. I include them because the discussion I hope to begin with you will be tough. We have to discuss trauma and alcohol and death. We have to talk about where we are, how we arrived here, and where we hope to go without making excuses and calling ourselves victims. I propose that the only way forward is to take full responsibility for ourselves and our present position and begin to tell a new story about ourselves. There is no easy or soft way of doing that.

You may also wonder, who am I to speak of such things. Let me tell you this about myself and then you can go on to read more, but here and now, let me say this: When I was eight years old, my father died of heart disease. It shattered my little world. Shortly afterwards a tyrannical teacher decided to discipline me. He had me stay after class. He then took me to the bottom of the stairs, took down my pants, and strapped my naked buttocks with a piece of heavy belting. That beating I probably could have lived with, as severe as it was. But he went further. He ran his hand over my buttocks, he said to see if they were warm enough after the whipping. It was that bit of humiliation that set the disciplining apart, that made it something *more*, more horrible, more demeaning.

Outside, standing alone in the schoolyard, crying and humiliated, I talked to the only person I could talk to: I talked to myself. I told myself that the only reason he was able to do that to me was because my father was dead. If I had had a father, someone to look out for me, he would never have dared to do what he had done.

A few months later I was sexually assaulted by a boy six or seven years older than I. Again, unable to talk to anyone because of the humiliation, I told myself that he would never have been able to do that to me if I had had a father.

Angry, unable to tell anyone, I took it out on everyone around me. Mostly boys, but girls too—I beat up people for no other reason than that they had a father. I did it because that was the story I was telling myself. I've told myself many stories over the years—that I was deprived because of poverty, that alcohol had ruined my childhood—and I acted out based upon the stories I was telling myself.

But here's the thing: I turned myself around. I was lucky. The horrible events I experienced when I was eight years old occurred before there were fancy theories floating around everywhere about trauma and victims. The problem with this latest story invented about us by *kiciwamanawak*—that we are a product of historical trauma—isn't just that it again makes us lesser people, people with a disorder. The problem is that it takes away our ability to do anything about it for ourselves. We can't fix colonization, we can't fix residential schools, we can't change *kiciwamanawak* opinions of us. If we are a product of historical trauma and so we're then victims, we are stuck in that story with no way of telling our way out of it.

And so, yes, I was lucky, because I never was diagnosed as or labelled a victim. When I was mature enough to realize that those events had caused some of my behaviours, I quit telling myself the story that the only reason things were not the way I wanted them to be was because my father had died. I forgave him for dying and went out and found new and better stories about who I was.

I changed the story about who I was and am.

And, speaking of history and story and defining who we are, throughout the text I have used the word *Indian*. Some people might have a problem with the word and find it offensive. We have all heard the story that Columbus was lost and thought he landed in India and mistook us for Indians. I prefer the explanation offered by Russell Means and the American Indian Movement (AIM):

Columbus was not lost, he knew where he was, and he called us *In Dios*, meaning "with God." The word is not as important as the story we tell about it. *Indian* is also a precise legal term found in our Treaties and the Canadian constitution.

The word *firewater* is a direct translation of the *nîhithaw* (Cree) word *iskotîwapoy*, the word we use for "alcohol"—*iskotîw* means "fire" and the suffix *apoy* means "liquid." The story I heard about how alcohol received its name tells of a time when the fur traders bartered with alcohol and were notorious for watering it down. To make sure that we were not being cheated, we would take a mouthful of the whiskey, then spit it in a fire. If the fire flared up, the whiskey was pure. If the fire went out, we knew we were being ripped off. We are still being sold firewater and we are still being ripped off, only today it's not for animal pelts—we pay for it with our lives and our health and our children's lives and futures.

ACKNOWLEDGEMENTS

The idea for this work began with an email from my son, Ray Johnson, containing an article about alcohol and anarchy. The authors of the article lamented that they could not organize as a group because alcohol kept getting in the way. The idea that alcohol was the reason why people did not overthrow their oppressors nagged at me, and I began to think about it and our situation as colonized peoples. Is alcohol the reason we do not push harder for self-government? It was an idea that would not go away. As a Crown prosecutor, I noted that the vast majority of people charged with offences were intoxicated at the time they committed the offence. When I started looking at alcohol in this larger context and realized it touched everything about us, I began to have discussions with my wife, Joan Johnson. Through many conversations with her and sharing information, the concept for this work began to grow. First, I wrote an article for *Justice as Healing* (University of Saskatchewan Native Law Centre) that I called "When He's Sober, He's a Good Guy."

ACKNOWLEDGEMENTS

That didn't satisfy me, and I kept thinking about our people and alcohol. I came across the work of Dr. James Irvine and was surprised to discover that the leading cause of death in this territory was injury. Knowing that alcohol was behind most injuries, I began to wonder, what was the death rate from alcohol. Dr. Irvine has become a friend and has assisted tremendously in pointing me to the available literature. The more I researched, the more frustrated I became. There are no direct statistics for alcohol and its damaging effects in our territory. At this point I wanted numbers to back up the arguments I was beginning to make in court that the justice system had a role to play in looking more closely at alcohol.

The work that became this book was influenced not only by discussions with my son and my wife, but also with my daughters Memegwans (Sarah) Johnson-Owl and her sister Anangons (Alita) Johnson-Owl. Provincial court judges Sid Robinson, Gerald Morin, Bob Lane, and Don Bird were also part of the discussion and each contributed in their own way. Russ Mirasty, Alan Adam, Noland Henderson, Alan (Spud) Morin, Tom Charles, Donald Caisse, Ray (Turk) Desjarlais, Myles Charles, Richard Thatcher, Peter Butt, and Duane Hunt all added their voices and their ideas. Neal McLeod, Solomon Ratt, and Simon Bird helped with getting the Cree words correctly spelled and used in the right context. A special thank you to Tracey Lindberg and Richard Van Camp for their contributions. Karen Clark contributed much to the formation and construction of the manuscript. While I thank everyone who contributed, I, of course, take full responsibility for all omissions and errors.

PART 1

KAYÂS: A LONG TIME AGO

WÎSAHKICÂHK'S LOST STORIES

Kayâs, *one day Wîsahkicâhk was watching television, and he saw an Indian story on there. But the story didn't seem right. It was all mixed up.*

He went to check the original.

He had it somewhere.

The Creator gave Wîsahkicâhk a whole bag of stories back at the beginning of time and he told Wîsahkicâhk, "Here, look after these, the people are going to need them to know how to live a good life, and they are going to need them when things get difficult."

But Wîsahkicâhk couldn't find them.

Man, he was in trouble now.

He lost the stories the Creator gave him.

So he went looking for them, and he saw Buffalo, way off in the distance, just one by himself. Wîsahkicâhk walked over to him and said, "Hey, paskwa mostos, my brother. Have you seen that bag of stories the Creator gave me? I think I lost them."

Buffalo shook his big shaggy head. He said, "Noooooooh, sorry, Wîsahkicâhk. I don't see much anymore. They keep me here in the park and people come to

look at me. I don't get around like I used to. Noooooooh, I
didn't see where you left your stories."

There was Wolf, running away from him.
Wîsahkicâhk shouted, "Hey, mahikan! My brother, stop,
wait. Why are you always running away?"

Wolf stopped and came back. "I try to stay away
from people now. Every time I come close, they shoot
at me or try to poison me. What can I do for you,
Wîsahkicâhk?"

"I lost that bag of stories the Creator gave me. You
didn't happen to see them, did you?"

"No, sorry, older brother," Wolf answered. "No, I'm
sorry, I never saw your stories."

Wîsahkicâhk kept looking. Next he saw Bear dig-
ging around in a garbage pit. He shouted down to him,
"Hey, maskwa, my brother. What are you doing down
there?"

Bear answered, "This is where I eat now. There's no
forest left, there's no berries."

"Oh well, I guess that's the way it is. You didn't by
chance happen to see where I left that bag of stories the
Creator gave me, now, did you?

"No, sorry, Wîsahkicâhk. I never saw them. But
maybe you never lost them. Maybe someone stole them
like they stole my claws and my gall bladder."

That made sense to Wîsahkicâhk. Of course, someone stole them. That must be what happened. That's
how they ended up on that television.

He looked up and there was Bald Eagle flying. He
yelled up at her, "Hey, mikisîw, my sister."

She circled around and around and slowly came
down. When she landed in a tree just above Wîsahkicâhk, he said, "Sister, you can see far. You can see

4

the future and you can see the past. Did you see who stole that bag of stories the Creator gave me back at the beginning of time?"

"Yes, I did, Wîsahkicâhk," she answered. "While you were watching television in the twentieth century Fox stole your stories."

"Ohhhhh yeah. That makes sense."

So Wîsahkicâhk went looking for Fox and he found him, and Fox had that bag of stories. He was dragging it around. Wîsahkicâhk knew he could never catch Fox. Fox was too fast, he could turn too quickly, and if Wîsahkicâhk chased him, maybe the stories would get hurt.

So he followed him and he found one of those stories. It had fallen out of the bag. Fox had dragged that bag of stories around for so long that he had worn a hole in it.

Wîsahkicâhk picked up that story. It was almost dead. Its fur was all matted and dirty, and it was hardly even breathing, It just lay there in Wîsah-kicâhk's hands with its eyes closed. It was the Dream Catcher story.

Wîsahkicâhk brushed the dirt off it and he blew on it. Blew a little bit of life on it.

Slowly that story began to revive.

Wîsahkicâhk blew on it some more.

Finally that little story opened its eyes. It wasn't completely strong yet. But Wîsahkicâhk had a plan.

He used that story to make a whole bunch of dream catchers. They weren't very good because the story was so weak. But they were good enough. He sold them and he sold his buckskin jacket that he didn't wear anymore, and he sold his moccasins, and he used that money to buy the biggest big-screen TV he could find.

Then he took that big-screen TV *into the forest and he plugged it into a currant bush.*

And then he hid and waited.

Sure enough.

Along came Fox.

Curious Fox. He stopped to watch that big TV, *and when he was completely hypnotized by it . . . Wîsah-kicâhk stole back the bag of stories so that the people would know again how to live a good life.*

PART 2

HOW ALCOHOL IS
KILLING MY PEOPLE

1. SO THE STORY GOES

tanisi ketayayak. Hello, Elders.
tanisi nimisak. Hello, my older sisters.
tanisi nistîsak. Hello, my older brothers.
tanisi nisimisak. Hello, all my younger
brothers and sisters.
tanisi kakithaw niwâhkomakinak.
Hello, all my relatives.

There is something important to talk about, something we have left out of our conversations, and now it is destroying us. There is a story that has been going around for a long time. The story is about the dirty, lazy, drunken Indian. The Queen's children have been telling this story about us ever since they came here. We were told this story when we went to residential schools, and though the media has somewhat toned it down as of late, this story is still repeated, and it is a story that we also tell to ourselves. It is the same story that is told about original peoples all over the world.

We once told our own stories about ourselves wherein we were the heroes. We were great hunters, providers, even warriors when need be. We were wise grandmothers and medicine people. We told stories about ourselves and about *mithosin kitaskinâw*—our beautiful land. The stories we told about ourselves and our beautiful land in fact had real effect. The stories connected us to the land and connected the land to us, and we became the same story.

But then the Queen's children came here and asked our ancestors if they could share this beautiful land with us. We adopted them in a ceremony of Treaty and they became our cousins.[1] Our name for them is *kiciwaman-awak*. It is a word that has no parallel in their language. It means all of us are cousins to all of them. *kiciwaman-awak* brought their own stories with them here. They brought the Jesus story and the money story, and they brought the alcohol story.

2. WHO AM I TO SPEAK?

My name is Harold Johnson and I am Cree from northern Saskatchewan, Treaty 6 territory. I want to share with you the little bit that I know about stories, and about alcohol and how the two work together to destroy us. I have not been asked to speak. No one said, "Harold, what do you think?" I speak as a citizen of the Woodland Cree peoples. I speak because what I am about to say is important for the people. I apologize if I speak out of turn without being asked. But I cannot sit silently any longer. Too many people have already died. There is too much suffering among our people. I have stood at too many gravesides and said goodbye to too many friends.

I grew up here on this land, the son of a trapper and fisherman.

I have spent time in the Canadian navy, worked as a logger and miner, raised a family, and have grandchildren. Twenty-five years ago I got tired of mining and went to university and studied law. I received a Bachelor of Laws degree from the University of Saskatchewan and a Master of Laws degree from Harvard University. I have worked on the defence side of criminal law and now I am employed as a Crown prosecutor in Saskatchewan.

I speak, however, only to my people, the Woodland Cree. I have no right to speak to anyone else. But if you hear my words and if these words help you, then take them and use them in a good way. If you cannot use them in a good way, then leave them here.

In our tradition a person does not speak, does not interfere, until he or she has been asked. We are not preachers. We do not proselytize. We do not take medicine to sick people and tell them, "Here, drink this. It will make you better." We each have our own understanding of our unique place in the universe. We get to our place of understanding through ceremonies, through suffering, through rationally interpreting our experience on this planet in relation to our own internal message.

Saulteaux Elder Danny Musqua once explained it to me like this: "You were a pure spirit traveling across the universe, just a dot of blue light, and you came across the Creator. The Creator was both spirit and physical at the same time. You said, 'I want to be like that,' and you came down to this earth to experience being physical and spirit at the same time. While you are here, you should focus on the Creator all the time. Never let anyone come between you and the Creator and never come between someone else and the Creator."

We each know that our life experience is ours alone. We each have our own interpretation of our place and our purpose here, and no one has a right to interfere in our understanding. We know that we each have our own understanding of our relationship with Creation.

We know that if we have medicine and someone needs it, it is up to them to ask for it. It is said that if they want it, they will crawl to come and get it. "Medicine," in our understanding, is not just roots and flowers and plants. It is much more than that. Medicine is in the rocks we use in Sweat Lodge ceremonies. It's in that Sundance Tree. It's in our thoughts and our actions.

We know that if we go around preaching and handing out medicine without being asked, there will be consequences, and maybe we won't like the results. Everything balances itself out eventually. The man who puts on a show—"Look at me! I am a great healer! I am a wise man! I am, I am, I am!"—will someday find out that he is just a man like everyone else. He will get knocked down.

I do not want to be the man who gets knocked down. But to those who say that we must be asked before we do anything, I reply: If you see an elderly woman fall into the campfire, do you wait for her to ask you for help? Or do you try to get her out of the fire as quickly as you can?

I cannot stay silent any longer. I cannot with good conscience bury another relative. I have now buried two brothers who were killed by drunk drivers. I cannot watch any longer as a constant stream of our relatives comes into the justice system because of the horrible things they did to each other while they were drunk. The suffering caused by alcohol, the kids with Fetal Alcohol Spectrum Disorder (FASD), the violence, the poverty, the abandoned children, the mental wards and the emergency rooms, the injuries and the illness and the loss of hope and the suicides have all piled up within me to the point that I must speak.

I must speak because so few are speaking. Our political leaders, our chiefs and councillors, the Assembly of First Nations, the Indian federations, the tribal council—all seem so silent. *kiciwamanawak* have turned and looked the other way. Their governments are silent, their churches are silent, their schools and hospitals are silent. Even their police officers who have to deal with alcohol everyday do not speak up. *kiciwamanawak* cannot speak about us and alcohol. They cannot use the words *Indian* and *alcohol* in the same sentence. If one of them were to speak up, they would be called racist and accused of stereotyping. Given the history between our peoples, racist is not something *kiciwamanawak* want to be called.

Why don't our leaders speak? Are our political leaders too embarrassed to say anything? What are they afraid of? Are they afraid that if they say something about the devastation caused by alcohol, people will point at us and call us names for being drunks? Are they afraid that someone will say, "See . . . it's true, they are just a bunch of dirty, lazy, drunken Indians"? And why don't we speak? Are we embarrassed and afraid too?

I apologize, *niwâhkomakanak*, I am about to drag this filthy, stinking subject out into the light where everyone can see it. It is my hope that the light kills it. I am going to speak without being asked because no one else is speaking and the silence needs to be broken.

If they point their fingers at us and say mean things about us, oh well, it can't be any worse than it already is.

3. THE DRUNKEN INDIAN STORY

When *kiciwamanawak* first came to our territory, they brought the Jesus story and the alcohol story and the money story, and we traded animal pelts with them for their money and their alcohol.

Ever since *kiciwamanawak* got here, they have been telling stories about 'the drunken Indian.' During the height of the fur trade, *kiciwamanawak* brought 50,000 gallons of liquor into our territory every year. More than a third of the freight in the North West Company canoes was ninety-pound kegs of rum. When they got the fire-water here, they diluted it with water and traded about 250,000 gallons. Our population at the time was about 120,000 people, including women and children.[2]

Duncan McGillivray worked for the North West Company. In his journal, dated 1794–95, is the following description of our people at a party:

> Men, women, and children promiscuously min-gle together and join in one diabolical clamour of singing, crying, fighting &c and to such excess do they indulge their love of drinking that all regard

for decency or decorum is forgotten—they expose themselves in the most indecent positions, leaving uncovered those parts which they carefully avoid in their sober moments, and the intercourse between the sexes, at any time but little restrained, is now indulged with the greatest freedom, for a chastity is not deemed a virtue among the tribes, they take very little pains to conceal their amours, especially when heated with liquor.[3]

Daniel Williams Harmon, a puritanical fur trader who also joined the North West Company in the early 1800s, went up to Dene territory and wrote in his diary:

To see a house full of drunken Indians, consisting of men, women and children, is a most unpleasant sight; for, in that condition, they often wrangle, pull each other by the hair, and fight. At some times, ten or twelve, of both sexes, may be seen, fighting each other promiscuously, until at last, they all fall on the floor, one upon another, some spilling rum out of a small kettle or dish, which they hold in their hands, while others are throwing up what they have just drunk. To add to this uproar, a number of children some on their mothers' shoulders, and others running about and taking hold of their clothes, are constantly bawling, the older ones, through fear that their parents may be stabbed, or that some other misfortune may befall them, in the fray. These shrieks of the children, form a very unpleasant chorus to the brutal noise kept up by their drunken parents, who are engaged in the squabble.[4]

3. THE DRUNKEN INDIAN STORY

Another story from a fur trader of that time tells:

> Every one knows the passion of the savages for this liquor, and the fatal effects that it produces on them.... The village or the cabin in which the savages drink brandy is an image of hell: fire [i.e., burning brands or coals flung by the drunkards] flies in all directions; blows with hatchets and knives make the blood flow on all sides; and all the place resounds with frightful yells and cries.... They roll about on the cinders and coals, and in blood.[5]

Alexander Henry the Younger, yet another early Canadian fur trader, wrote: "We may truly say that liquor is the root of all evil in the North West.... The Indians continued drinking. About ten o'clock I was informed that old Crooked Legs had killed his young wife.... By sunrise every soul of them was raving drunk – even the children."[6]

In 1788 Benjamin Franklin wrote in his autobiography as follows:

> As those people are extremely apt to get drunk, and, when so, are very quarrelsome and disorderly, we strictly forbade the selling any liquor to them; and when they complained of this restriction, we told them that if they would continue sober during the treaty, we would give them plenty of rum when business was over. They promised this, and they kept their promise, because they could get no liquor; and the treaty was conducted very orderly, and concluded to mutual satisfaction.

They then claimed and received the rum; this was in the afternoon: they were near one hundred men, women, and children, and were lodged in temporary cabins, built in the form of a square, just without the town. In the evening, hearing a great noise among them, the commissioners walked out to see what was the matter. We found they had made a great bonfire in the middle of the square; they were all drunk, men and women, quarreling and fighting. Their dark-colored bodies, half naked, seen only by the gloomy light of the bonfire, running after and beating one another with firebrands, accompanied by their horrid yellings, formed a scene the most resembling our ideas of hell that could well be imagined; there was no appeasing the tumult, and we retired to our lodging. At midnight a number of them came thundering at our door, demanding more rum, of which we took no notice. The next day, sensible they had misbehaved in giving us that disturbance, they sent three of their old counselors to make their apology. The orator acknowledged the fault, but laid it upon the rum; and then endeavored to excuse the rum by saying: *"The Great Spirit, who made all things, made everything for some use, and whatever use he designed anything for, that use it should always be put to. Now, when he made rum, he said, 'Let this be for the Indians to get drunk with,' and it must be so."* And, indeed, if it be the design of Providence to extirpate these savages in order to make room for cultivators of the earth, it seems not improbable that rum may be the appointed means. It has already annihilated all the tribes who formerly inhabited the sea-coast.[7]

The stories of 'the drunken Indian' that *kiciwaman-awak* tell about us haven't changed much in the last 200 years. I was working in Geneva, Switzerland, in 1995, as an intern for the International Labour Office. I met a man in a bar and we were having a beer in the afternoon. When I told the man I was an Indian, he was very concerned that I was drinking. He was genuinely afraid that I was going to become a raving drunk and possibly scalp him because the only stories he'd heard about us and alcohol were similar to the ones above.

4. A LITTLE BIT MORE HISTORY TO HELP PUT IT IN PERSPECTIVE

We have known for a long time about the destructiveness of alcohol. In 1875, when *kiciwamanawak* sent people onto the prairies to survey telegraph lines across Cree territory, our ancestors met them and turned them back. We told them not to come here until we had a Treaty. *kiciwamanawak* knew that we were the most powerful military power here. They could not force their way across the land, so they sent the missionary George McDougall to talk to us and find out what we wanted. We met with him and sent a letter back with him to the Treaty commissioner. We told the commissioner what we wanted. On that list was a ban on alcohol. We said, "When we see it we want to drink it, and it destroys us; when we do not see it we do not think about it."[8]

In 1876 we met with Treaty Commissioner Alexander Morris and negotiated Treaty 6. In this adoption ceremony, the Queen's children were given the right to be here.[9] They were given the right to have farms and to use the land to the depth of a plough. They were given the right to use the trees and take the minerals. The Treaty commissioner talked for a long time, and then our ancestors went off by themselves to discuss things. They took the interpreter with them. When they came back to the negotiations, they had a list of demands. They knew that *kiciwamanawak* understood things better if they were written down. On that written list of demands, we again asked for a ban on alcohol.[10]

It was written into our Treaty that our people would be protected from the evil influences of alcohol throughout the land we shared, and that no alcohol would be allowed on our reserves. I've put a copy of this Treaty at the back of this book for you to read for yourself.

kiciwamanawak tried to honour the Treaty promise they made by making it illegal for our people to have alcohol. If caught with it, we were fined. Then in 1967 there was a man named Drybones who was charged for possession of alcohol.[11] The case went all the way to the Supreme Court of Canada. Just before this case, the Government of Canada had passed a law called the Canadian Bill of Rights. This law said that everyone was equal. The Supreme Court used this new law to say that Drybones had a human right to drink alcohol and that it was discriminatory to not allow Indigenous peoples to drink. They struck down the law that said it was illegal for our people to have alcohol or go into a bar. The Supreme Court did not ask us about these changes and this new law. The judges did not look at the Treaties or the negotiations that led to the Treaties. They decided what would be best for us without talking to us first.

So the Indian Act was thus changed, and now it is up to each First Nation to decide if its reserve is going to allow alcohol. Some of our reserves are dry, while others are not. The same argument is taking place today as in the *Drybones* decision. When a person is charged with having alcohol on-reserve and the case comes before the provincial court, defence lawyers frequently argue that the law is discriminatory because white people and other non-Indigenous peoples in Canada are allowed to drink. Judges reluctantly uphold the band's bylaw and give only the minimum fines. Elders in these communities laugh at the justice system because the fine for breaching the band's bylaw is $100 and the going price for a bootleg bottle of whiskey is $125.

When our ancestors sent the message to the Treaty commissioner in 1876, they knew that alcohol was destroying us. They also knew that it was *kiciwamanawak* who had brought the firewater here and that it was their responsibility to make sure it didn't destroy people. Alcohol is still destroying us and it is still *kiciwamanawak* who are bringing it here. That part of the Treaty that was insisted upon by our ancestors is now almost completely ignored.

5. A TIME BEFORE ALCOHOL KILLED OUR PEOPLE

A n Elder described the evolution of drinking in his community. He said that back in the 1950s, there were some people who had sold their Treaty rights and were legally able to go into the local bar. Some people who lived on the reserve would ask those disenfranchised people to buy beer for them. He said drinking was something that happened once in a while, but you had to be careful because you didn't want the Indian agent to find out. Then in 1960 the law changed in Saskatchewan, and Indians were allowed to vote and go into the bar. It was a few years later that women were allowed in the bar. He remembered men being in the bar and women waiting outside.

The big change came when the Anglo Rouyn Mine opened in 1966. He said there was a constant party on the reserve as miners supplied alcohol to women. The party went twenty-four hours a day as day-shift miners were replaced by night-shift miners. There was another group of men in the community who also lived in a bunkhouse.

The Smoke Jumpers parachuted in to fight forest fires. These men also had a constant party going and again it was to get women drunk. The third group of men preying on Indian women was the tourists. Rich Americans flew into La Ronge to go fishing. They did not bring their wives and families with them. They did, however, bring hard liquor, which was otherwise not available.

Elders from another community in this territory said they had no advice about drinking. In their day there was very little alcohol because it was banned on the reserve. Drinking did not really become a problem until the law changed. They had no teachings, nothing to look back upon, no cultural stories to help people who were asking them what to do about increased violence caused by alcohol.

It seems that serious problems with alcohol did not begin in our territory until well into the 1960s. This is not a long time ago. Most Elders remember a time before alcohol killed half our people.

6. GOING TO THE GRAVEYARD

In our territory the leading cause of death is injury. In 2011 injury accounted for 23.4 per cent of all deaths (see Figure 6.1). The death rate from injury for the entire province of Saskatchewan was 6 per cent and was that high only because of the death rate in the North (see Figure 6.2).[12]

These deaths from injuries in our communities are caused by suicide, car accidents, snowmobile accidents, drowning, stabbing, shooting, beating, house fires, and freezing to death (see Figure 6.3). And behind these deaths by injury is one thing, and that is alcohol.

We know that there is a very strong connection between the use of alcohol and suicide.[13] We know that most stabbings, shootings, and beatings occur during drunken rages. Drinking and driving, whether it's done in a car or on a snowmobile, a quad, or a boat, frequently ends in either injury or tragedy—often both—and we end up at the graveside, saying goodbye to yet another of our relatives.

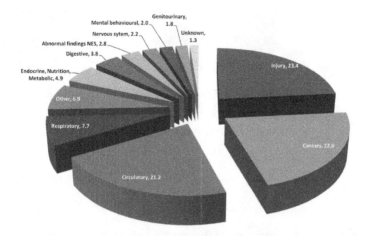

FIGURE 6.1. Causes of death in Northern Saskatchewan communities, 1998–2007. SOURCE: Irvine et al., "Northern Saskatchewan Health Indicators Report."

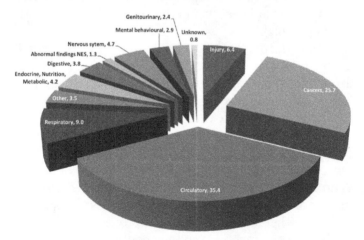

FIGURE 6.2. Causes of death in the Province of Saskatchewan, 1998–2007. SOURCE: Irvine et al., "Northern Saskatchewan Health Indicators Report."

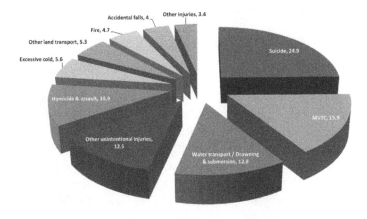

FIGURE 6.3. Types of injury leading to death in Northern Saskatchewan communities, 1998–2007. SOURCE: SaskHealth 2009, prepared by Population Health Unit, September 2010 (www.populationhealthunit.ca).

Alcohol is known to cause heart disease.[14] Many of the men my age who drank hard all their lives are now falling over dead from heart attacks. There is a story that has been going around that red wine is good for the heart, that a glass a day is good for you. The story is repeated and repeated, but I suspect that the people who sell red wine made up the story.[15]

What they neglect to mention when they talk about drinking red wine to preserve the heart is that alcohol causes cancer.[16] Alcohol is considered to be carcinogenic and is strongly associated with an increased risk for certain types of cancer such as colorectal cancer, breast cancer, some cancers of the central nervous system, and cancers of the larynx, pharynx, esophagus, and liver.[17] Alcohol not only increases the risk of getting cancer, it also reduces the length of time cancer may be present but is inactive in the body; it increases cancer's severity,

27

and increases the number of tumours or types of cancer present.[18]

Dr. Gregory Taylor, Canada's Chief Public Health Officer, wrote in his 2015 report:

> Our understanding of the dose-dependent health effects of alcohol continues to evolve. Recent research questions the health benefits of low to moderate alcohol consumption. Studies suggest that women are at increased risk for breast cancer even at a low level of one drink per day. The international Agency for Research on Cancer's *World Cancer Report 2014* and the Canadian Cancer Society state "that there is no safe limit of alcohol consumption when it comes to cancer prevention."[19]

Alcohol use is linked to over 200 different diseases, conditions, and types of injuries.[20] Globally, alcohol kills more people than lung cancer and HIV/AIDS combined.[21]

We can put these three things together—that alcohol is behind the extreme rate of injury in our territory, that alcohol causes heart disease, and that alcohol is strongly associated with many cancers—and add to those three known facts these other facts: that children who do not receive proper nutrition when they are young (because their parents are drinking) have shorter life expectancies as a result; that people who drink excessively are less likely to eat properly and take care of their health, and are going to have shorter lives; and that there is a known impact of alcohol on diabetes. If we add all these facts together, the cumulative effects are that every second person in our territory is going to die an alcohol-related death. This means, then, that *50 per cent of all deaths in our territory are alcohol-related.*

In any other situation, we would call this a crime against humanity. If the Israelis were to kill half the Palestinians, or if white Americans were to shoot half the population of black Americans in the United States, the world would be outraged. But half of our people can die from something completely preventable and no one says a word.

niwâhkomakanak, it is up to us. *kiciwamanawak* are not going to do anything to help us. They never have, so why would they start now?

7. THE ROYAL COMMISSION ON ABORIGINAL PEOPLES AND THE SUPREME COURT

Some people have had the courage to speak about Aboriginal peoples and alcohol. The 1996 Royal Commission on Aboriginal Peoples (RCAP) was established after the Oka conflict in the early 1990s. It was an extraordinary review of our situation. It cost millions of dollars and took years to complete. The commissioners had to deal with alcohol. It was too blatant a subject to ignore.

The commissioners first set out the harm caused by alcohol as follows:

> Excessive consumption of alcohol has serious physical health consequences; it increases the risk of heart disease, cirrhosis and liver disease, gastritis and gastro-intestinal cancers, hepatitis and fetal alcohol syndrome. Its social and emotional correlates include accidents, suicides, family violence and breakdown, unemployment, criminal

behaviour and, to apply a concept from pediatrics, "failure to thrive."[22]

The commissioners quoted my friend Winston McKay, who said, "Twenty-three years ago, I woke up one morning and knew I was going to die unless I quit drinking, so I quit.... Of the men of my generation who were my working and drinking companions, most are dead in violence, in accidents or from alcohol-related diseases."[23]

The commissioners argued back and forth about this study and that study and which might be correct. Were we drinking more or were we drinking less? Then they said, "In any case, the widely held belief that most Aboriginal people consume excessive amounts of alcohol on a regular basis appears to be incorrect."[24]

The Royal Commission obviously got it wrong. I recently heard a kid in a northern community refer to the day that the band issued cheques as the "day of the zombies." There were so many intoxicated people staggering around his community that it reminded him of the zombie apocalypse. There were so many people drunk in his community that he was afraid to go outside to play.

The problem with intoxicated people is so severe that we have communities where it is common to bolt steel brackets to the wall for a 2 × 4 wooden bar to hold the door shut to stop the intoxicated people from coming around and kicking it down. We frequently see signs posted in community businesses that warn people not to go there when intoxicated. A typical sign that I see frequently reads as follows: "Any persons showing signs of intoxication will be asked to leave immediately. Failure to comply will result in the RCMP being notified immediately." This is not normal but it is here, in our communities.

So I think the commissioners got it wrong. Many Aboriginal people do consume excessive amounts of alcohol on a regular basis. In their multi-volume report the commission gave a little more than eight pages to the problem of alcohol, and one of those pages was a chart. They had the courage to look at alcohol, but they did not have the courage to look it in the face. They did not count the dead. They did not do the math. How many of us have to die from alcohol before we add up the numbers?

The Supreme Court of Canada in the case of *R. v. Gladue* looked at the number of our relatives who end up in jail. Everyone knows that Aboriginal people are overrepresented in jails. This has been going on for a long time. Many people have suggested that the reason so many of our relatives go to jail is because the justice system discriminates against us. From my experience, it is true. There is a built-in bias against us in the justice system.[25] But that discrimination alone doesn't account for the high numbers of our people in custody.

In *R. v. Gladue* the Supreme Court agreed that the number of Aboriginal people in jail was too high and told the lower court judges to look at our background. They said:

> The background factors which figure prominently in the causation of crime by aboriginal offenders are by now well known. Years of dislocation and economic development have translated, for many aboriginal peoples, into low incomes, high unemployment, lack of opportunities and options, lack or irrelevance of education, substance abuse,

> loneliness, and community fragmentation. These
> and other factors contribute to a higher incidence
> of crime and incarceration.[26]

What the court was saying is that we commit more crimes because of our background: poor people commit more crimes, unemployed people commit more crimes, uneducated people commit more crimes.

From my experience in the courts for nearly twenty years, I would estimate that about 95 per cent of the people charged and convicted of crimes were intoxicated at the time they committed the offence. In that time I have not met many people who could be called "criminal." Mostly I've met people who drank too much and did something stupid. In fact, when someone comes to court charged with a crime that was committed while they were sober, the prosecutor will often tell the judge, or, in other ways, suggest to the judge, that "this person is so bad that they did this horrible thing while they were actually sober."

We have to ask ourselves: Are we drunks because we are poor, or are we poor because we drink? Do we drink because we don't have a job, or do we not have a job because we drink? Do we drink because our communities are fragmented, or are our communities fragmented because we drink? Do we drink because we come from broken homes, or do we have broken homes because we drink?

Alcohol has been used against us—a key tool of colonialism since *kiciwamanawak* arrived here. As Duncan McGillivray of the North West Company wrote in his journal in the eighteenth century: "The love of Rum is their first inducement to industry; they undergo every hardship and fatigue to procure a skinfull of this delicious beverage, and when a Nation becomes addicted to drinking, it affords a strong presumption that they will soon become excellent hunters."[27]

Drinking is part of the colonial experience. Self-induced intoxication is self-induced colonization. By drinking, we participate in our own colonization. We take all the negative ideas that *kiciwamanawak* brought here and we take them into ourselves. We are born again as the colonizer through the ceremony of drinking.

8. FOUR MODELS

I. THE VICTIM MODEL

The Victim Model of dealing with alcoholism is to blame colonization, to blame the residential schools, to blame poverty and failed government policy. Although these circumstances are, without a doubt, significant factors, this model offers no solutions. It attempts to explain the reasons but ends up creating excuses and continuing the problem.

If we believe that the only reasons for our problems rest with colonization, we can never fix our problems, because we cannot go back and fix colonization. We cannot go back and change residential schools.

We have to be very careful of these people who insist on dealing with the alcohol problem only by seeing it through the Victim Model—by creating stories about us that are only about victimhood. If we listen to their story and accept what they say, we will be forever trapped in our present situation.

Why is this the case? Because if the problem is caused by someone else, if the problem is *kiciwamanawak* government or *kiciwamanawak* police, or anyone else other than ourselves, then we can never fix it. We can never fix the problem if the problem is not ours. If we allow ourselves to believe the victim story and we live by it, we become victims, and victims can never fix their own situations.

If we are victims, if our situation is entirely caused by *kiciwamanawak* actions or inactions, then it is up to *kiciwamanawak* to fix it. They have to either act or stop acting. If we follow this line of reasoning, then we have to wait for them, or compel them, or pressure them, or embarrass them, or vote for the other political party, the one that promises to help.

We've been waiting for over a hundred years, since the making of Treaty, for *kiciwamanawak* to do what they promised at Treaty. I predict that we could wait another hundred years and the situation would be the same. Even if the problem belonged to *kiciwamanawak*, even if they were at fault, why would they want to do anything about it?

Those *kiciwamanawak* who believe the story that they are the sole problem, that our situation comes only from the history of colonization, and who then try to do something to change it—they become the keepers of the Victim Model, and, by doing so, they make things worse. And if we believe the victim story that we are powerless, that the problem belongs to *kiciwamanawak*, then when *kiciwamanawak* come around to fixing our problem, I bet we are not going to like whatever solution they propose.

II. THE GRIEF AND TRAUMA MODEL

The Grief and Trauma Model is part of the Victim Model. In this newer version of the older Victim Model, the problem with alcohol in our lives stems from the fact that Aboriginal peoples have been subjected to a history of trauma, going back to residential schools and even earlier in the history of colonization. Again, this model offers an accurate explanation, in many ways, for the problems with alcohol in our communities, but it too fails to offer any solutions.

What we've been told about alcohol and trauma is backwards. Research shows that post-traumatic stress disorder (PTSD) is often brought on by drinking.[28] Alcohol and PTSD are related.[29] Alcohol is not only associated with the onset of PTSD, it is also known to cause more severe symptoms. A person might experience a traumatic event and not have any problems with it until they start drinking. So in this sense, alcohol can cause PTSD even though many people who experience the symptoms of PTSD use alcohol to cope with those symptoms.

The trauma most often pointed at to explain our destructive drinking habits is the residential school. Yes, it happened. Yes, horrible things occurred there. Yes, many people who attended residential schools were severely traumatized.[30] But traumatic events did not end when the residential schools were closed. Alcohol creates its own trauma. More often than not, the trauma our relatives experience occurs as a result of excessive drinking. So, while trauma might cause drinking, it is more often that drinking causes trauma.

As an example, I know a young man from a community near here who had a girlfriend. The two of them were having a few relationship problems and had walked away from the community along the highway to a nearby river. They were standing on the bridge, consuming alcohol, and having a heated discussion. The girl decided to punish the young man by committing suicide—she jumped in front of a semi-truck that was passing by just then.

The young man was devastated and confused by what he had seen. He remained with her smashed body for several hours before the police and ambulance arrived. The experience haunted him, and he went to talk to an aunt for advice. She told him, "Go get good and drunk and let it go."

So he did.

He drank as much as he could for as long as he could. He woke up one morning in his car. The police were knocking on the window. They were investigating a hit and run. They found the victim's DNA under the young man's car. Sometime during the night he had run over his cousin and killed him. His grief over his girlfriend's senseless suicide was now doubled with his grief over the death of a cousin he was close to. At that moment, he quit drinking.

Trauma, grief, and drinking seem to go together in our communities. We stand at the gravesides of our dead relatives and experience pain. We want to avoid pain and so we drink, and with our drinking more people end up dead, and we stand again at another graveside and again experience pain. We live in a cycle of pain and grief and trauma and more pain and more grief again and again and again. But recognizing this Grief and Trauma Model has not fixed this cycle for us.

I asked earlier, do we drink because we are poor, or are we poor because we drink? Do we drink because of the conditions we live in, or do we live in these conditions because we drink? The answers to all such questions are both yes and no. Neither is the cause or the result; it is just a repeating cycle of alcohol and despair.

It's like we are on a fast-flowing river and caught in a large back eddy.[31] If we stay in the eddy we continue to go in circles. We have choices: stay where we are, paddle hard and get out into the main current, or climb up on the shore. The main current is dominant society going by, with all the jobs. It's fast flowing and no one knows exactly where it is going. The land we know about—that is the trapline and hunting and gathering. Earth is our mother. When our feet are firmly on the earth we are safe.

In that back eddy, in the swirl of drinking, and being and repeating, explained to us through the Grief and Trauma Model, the party never ends. My younger brother Garry was caught in it. He liked to party. He also liked to go to his trapline and was quite skilled in the bush, a good hunter and trapper and fisherman who knew his way around out here. But when he was in town, he liked to drink and smoke dope. He liked the party, he liked all his friends who showed up with a case of beer or a bag of pot, and when he had money he bought the beer and the pot and shared with his friends.

One night he was walking home from babysitting at his daughter's. She'd offered him money for a taxi, but he refused. To him, that was a waste of money. It wasn't that far to walk, only a couple of kilometres. He was about halfway home when a car came off the road and hit him. He lived only a few minutes afterwards. The driver never stopped, kept going, most likely because he had been drinking and so was afraid.

We buried him. We said our goodbyes at the funeral, held each other up, tried to remember the best parts of his life. For the most part, we didn't care who the driver was. What he or she did, he or she will have to live with. We were concerned only with Garry and his children and grandchildren.

After the funeral one of my nephews put up a cross at the site where Garry had been killed, something to mark the spot, something with which to remember him. This is a place people frequently walk past, going from one part of the community to another.

Full bottles of beer began to show up at the cross: people walking by with a case and leaving one for Garry. "Here's a beer for you, buddy." Marijuana joints were left in the same way: "Here, Garry, here's a hoot for you."

And other people would come by and drink the beer. "Hey, Garry, thanks for the beer."

"Hey, Garry, thanks for the hoot." And they would smoke the marijuana someone else had left.

Even after he was dead—even after we buried him, shed our tears, and hugged each other—the party continued.

I am going to suggest that we have to change our story before we can fix the alcohol problem. But it's a very powerful story that can go beyond the grave, and it is going to take a long time and a lot of effort before we change that story.

We are not going to change the story through the justice system. Garry's life and the person who drove while drunk and killed Garry—their lives won't change, no matter how many people we send to jail, or for how long we send them there. Neither does it matter what conditions we put in probation orders. Nothing changes. We fly into remote communities and when we get there we see the same people coming to court, charged with the same offences over and over and over again. And on the other side of the courtroom, there is a judge and a prosecutor and defence lawyer and a clerk, and they are doing the same things over and over and over again.

I cannot count the number of times I have heard an accused in court say that the reason they breached a condition of release that required them to stay sober was because someone died. They were on probation, or on bail with conditions to refrain from the consumption of alcohol, because of something they did, or were alleged to have done, while drinking, and then they went and got drunk and got themselves arrested. When I see them, they are sitting in court with their heads down.

Someone asks them, "So, what happened, you were doing so good?" And the reply is, "My grandma died." Or, "My dad died." Or, "My sister got killed."

To them, it's a total answer. But we have to read between the words. We have to imagine the grief and the pain, and the need to not feel that anymore.

Alcohol promises to drown grief and pain. But it doesn't. It just puts those terrible feelings aside, and when we sober up, the pain and grief are there again.

Our traditional way of dealing with death is to grieve for one year. A year is a long time—one complete cycle, a spring, a summer, an autumn, and a winter. At the end of the year we hold a memorial, at which we let go. There is a ceremony called "Wiping the Tears" that we go through to mark the end of grief. At the memorial we often take all those things left by the deceased that we have kept, those precious little articles that mean so much to us, and we give them away. We let go.

We understand that to grieve, to constantly cry and be sad, to walk around in sorrow—all that keeps the dead person's spirit here. We understand that to keep a spirit close for too long is not a good thing. The spirit needs to move on, to go to the other side and be with its relatives over there. By giving away those precious little things that we have kept, we let go of our relative's spirit at the same time.

A year of grief is a long journey. It is very painful and difficult, but we do get through it. When we come out the other end, we are not the same as when we began the journey. We are changed. Every death of a close relative changes us, and with each journey of grief we become a different person. We may become stronger, or quieter, or closer to our remaining relatives. If the person who died was the head of the family, our siblings might turn to us for leadership and guidance. When we lose a partner, we are forced to become both father and mother to our children.

But if we never complete the journey, if we get drunk instead and try to avoid it, we become stuck in grief. If we do not go through the whole year and experience it all—all the emotions, all the pain, the sorrow, the loneliness—then grief waits for us. As soon as we sober up, there it is, waiting. There is no way around grief. The only way past it is through it. We have to experience it and experience it fully before it goes away.

Remember Elder Danny Musqua's words: You were a pure spirit traveling across the universe, just a dot of blue light, and you came across the Creator. The Creator was both spirit and physical at the same time. You said, "I want to be like that," and you came down to this earth to experience being physical and spirit at the same time.

Grief and pain and sorrow are part of the experience of being a human. We go through those hardships in order to grow. Hardship should make us stronger, not weaker. But if we avoid the pain, if we try to drown it, and hide away from it in a bottle, we deprive ourselves of the chance to grow. We get stuck in the back eddy of despair, of grief and trauma, repeating it endlessly.

When my mother died, I went to an Elder for help. He gave me good advice. He said to be strong and look after my other relatives, who would be in need of someone to help hold them up. He said that by my helping others, my own pain would be easier to carry. When the grave-side ceremony was over, I helped my mother's cousin, who was quite old and frail, to walk back to her son's car. On the way she told me, "You are very strong, it used to be long ago, everyone was like that."

niwâhkomakanak, we have become weak. We have become afraid of normal things like death. There was a time when death was understood as the passing from one world to the next. We understood that we buried a body, or put it on a scaffold, but the spirit travelled to a place where all our relatives waited. In our traditional stories, death is not something to be afraid of. It is something to get ready for.

I don't know anyone anymore who is getting ready for their own death. It's coming. Everyone knows it. Can't do anything about it. We are mortal. We are going to die. So what's going to happen in those last minutes? How are we going to be? Are we going to face it, accept it, or are we going to get drunk and try to avoid it? I hope that we instantly sober up at the moment of death. It would be embarrassing to arrive in the new place still drunk, if, upon meeting our grandpa and grandma and aunts and uncles who went before us, we staggered and slurred our words and behaved like a clown.

To summarize the Victim and Trauma models of dealing with alcohol's harmful impact, they fail because their explanations are too simple. They try to explain something as complex as life and death and human emotions as mere cause and effect. They suggest that people turn to alcohol because of social conditions and trauma, without recognizing that at the same time, alcohol abuse causes those social conditions and often results in trauma.

The life and death and well-being of our people are matters that are far too important to leave to sociological hypotheses and liberal ideologies. These experts don't live with us. They either don't know or they fail to think about life as a complete experience. *niwâhkomakanak*, you know what is going on because you live in the communities. You know because it is your relatives, the people whom you love, who are suffering.

III. THE MEDICAL MODEL

We've tried to understand and treat the problems of alcohol by telling stories of victimhood (Victim Model) and of historical trauma (Grief and Trauma Model). There is also the standard Medical Model, which treats alcoholism as a disease. The treatment is to quit drinking with the use of support groups, a twelve-step program, surrendering oneself to something higher, and sheer willpower, and slowly, with time, the cravings should diminish and eventually stop.

The idea of treating alcoholism as a disease is a little misleading. Even though it kills a lot of people, it is not the same as smallpox, for instance. We have referred to alcoholism as a disease so that we could get our heads around the problem without blaming the alcoholic. Before we considered it a disease, we thought it was a moral problem or a willpower problem. Calling it a disease helped us to search for solutions without putting all the blame on the person, who was obviously unable to change on his or her own.

The problem with calling alcoholism a disease is that it takes control away from the alcoholic. If it is a disease like muscular dystrophy or measles or tuberculosis, then the person cannot do anything about it; that's just the way it is, a matter of chance or bad luck. We have been telling the alcoholic that the solution is that they have to quit drinking completely and never drink again as long as they live, and if they have trouble doing that, they should seek out a higher power to help them, and if they follow the twelve steps recommended by Alcoholics Anonymous and it still doesn't work, then they are not being honest enough.[32]

We might be better off calling alcoholism an "injury." Addictions and poor health from overconsumption are similar to repetitive strain, like carpal tunnel syndrome, where we use a particular muscle too much in a poor way and injure ourselves as a result. Excessive drinking in binges over a long period of time causes damage to our brains and other organs like the liver. No matter how serious the damage that's done, we still cannot call it a disease. Because here's the thing: like a sprained muscle, it starts to get better as soon as we quit using it. Leprosy doesn't work this way, and neither does cancer.

The difference between calling addiction a disease and calling it an injury is in how the person who has it deals with it. If the person says, "I have a disease. It's God's will. There is nothing I can do about it," then their power is taken away from them. If the person says instead, "I drank so much, so often, that I injured myself," then they are in a position to do something about it. It is something within their control.

The difference between calling the use of alcohol a disease and calling it an injury will have an impact upon how we drink. If a person is drinking and saying to themselves, "If I drink too much, too often, there is a possibility that I will injure myself," the possibility exists for them to be more careful about how often and how much they drink. If, on the other hand, they are drinking and saying to themselves, "This is a disease called alcoholism and I'm predisposed to it because of my family history or my people's shared history," then their view is fatalistic and they are less likely to modify their drinking because, after all, a disease is a matter of genetic destiny (there's no avoiding it; it's in your genes)—sheer bad luck—or it's God's will.

The biggest shortcoming with the Medical Model of approaching alcohol as a disease is not how it treats or fails to treat alcohol dependency. The problem with alcohol is that people who are not addicted to it, people like the person who ran over my brother, simply drink too much at times and then make poor decisions. Based upon the number of people I see in court who are charged with offences committed while drinking, I estimate that among that population of drinkers, only about 15 to 20 per cent are at the stage where they have drunk too much, too often, and, in doing so, have rewired their brains to the point that they are compulsively and obsessively addicted to alcohol. The Medical Model doesn't account for the 80 to 85 per cent of people experiencing problems with alcohol. This model, therefore, the one that tells a story of alcohol and disease, fails to help our greater community with problems of alcohol. The person who ran over Garry was not addicted to alcohol. He or she did drink excessively that one night, but that was one night too many.

The Medical Model fails most dramatically when we examine its success rate. It doesn't have one. The number of people who quit drinking as a result of going to a treatment centre is about 2 to 6 per cent.[33] The Alcoholics Anonymous twelve-step method works best for middle-aged, middle-class males who are prone to guilt and who are the first-born or only child.[34] This is the method upon which most treatment centres rely. This is where the courts send people who are placed on probation orders or conditional sentences. This is where Indian Child and Family Services sends the parents of children they have apprehended as a condition to getting their children back. This is the solution that many of us recommend to our relatives when they ask us what they should do about their problems.

We frequently hear from our elected leaders that we need more treatment centres: we need treatment centres closer to our communities so that people don't have to travel so far, we need more treatment centres so that the waiting times are shorter. We have come to depend upon this one, single solution, and it doesn't work for 94 to 98 per cent of the people who either are sent there or who go there in one last attempt to get their lives back in order.

We have to find a better way. Somehow we have to turn our communities into treatment centres, so that the whole community becomes involved in finding healthy alternatives.

IV. THE LAW ENFORCEMENT MODEL

We have known that the Law Enforcement Model—that of courts and judges and prosecutors and jails—has not worked for about a thousand years or at least for as long as we have had the common law. We can be sure that the earliest cases decided in a castle by the first judges of the assizes courts had to deal with people who drank too much and committed wrongs. Hence, we have the old proverb: "He that killeth a man drunk, sober shall be hanged."[35]

I haven't been involved with the Law Enforcement Model for that long a time—a thousand years is a long time—but I have been a defence counsel and a prosecutor and thus have spent the last twenty years in court, dealing with this model. Over that course of time, I have seen our relatives brought, often in handcuffs, time and again to answer for something that they did; and most of these times, the person charged did what they did when they were drunk.

I know a woman who really loved her family. She got drunk with her daughter, and sometime during the night the two of them got into a fight. The daughter attacked the mother, and during the fight the mother stabbed the daughter in the throat with a knife.

The daughter had a child when she was young, whom the mother had raised. Now that boy has to live with the fact that his mother was killed by his grandmother, by the woman who raised him, who loved him, who took care of him. That whole family is in turmoil, devastated by a few minutes of drunken violence. The consequences will be played out for generations yet to come.

The justice system becomes involved, and the story of that family has to be retold in the story of the law. In law a person is responsible for their actions when they are intoxicated unless it can be proven that they were so intoxicated that their brain was incapable of making decisions. In most cases, drunkenness cannot be used as a defence. The person is taken to have intended doing what they did.

So, as told in the law story, the mother intended to stab the daughter to death. But everyone who knows the mother knows that she would never do so if she were sober; everyone knows that it was the alcohol, not the mother. She loved her children and her grandchildren. Her only real crime was that she started drinking. She knew that horrible things can happen when alcohol is involved, because she'd experienced many of them herself during her lifetime, but she drank that night anyway. But she did not intend to kill her daughter. The law story makes it so.

And the law story changes constantly. For instance, governments who want to be re-elected will make the law harsher if the politicians believe that the people who vote for them want them to be tough on crime. The Criminal Code is constantly being amended, but the amendments are driven more by political interests than by concepts of justice.

The law of Canada is whatever the Supreme Court says it is. The government might make law, but the Supreme Court gets the final say when it interprets the law, and the interpretations are constantly changing.

There may appear to be a conflict between the Supreme Court and the government when the court strikes down a law made by the government, but when it comes to alcohol, it seems that they are both in the same story. In that story, alcohol is an everyday experience.

On the northern court circuit, the judge and the prosecutor and the defence lawyer (usually Legal Aid, but sometimes private lawyers as well) fly into remote communities once or twice a month. The court party is met by the local Royal Canadian Mounted Police (RCMP) and driven from the airport, if the community has an airport, and, at other times, from the lake, if the court party flew in on a bush plane on floats or skis. All are driven to a community hall, where court is held. We hold court all day and often late into the evening. We spend an entire day dealing with people who were drunk when they committed the offence with which they were charged. It's a triple-A court; that is, we are nothing more than Alcohol Aftermath Administrators.

I say this because the most common charges we deal with are assaults, domestic violence, and occasionally sexual assaults, and alcohol is almost always involved. People are also frequently charged with resisting arrest or assaulting a police officer. The person charged often doesn't remember the incident. They were so intoxicated that they blacked out. It is common for a person charged with assaulting police to apologize to the officers the next morning when they awaken in cells. Depending upon the seriousness of the assault, the sincerity of the apology, and the character of the officer, these charges are sometimes dropped before they come to court.

After a day in court, after doing what the Law Enforcement Model requires, after hearing over and over again that "when he's sober, he's a good guy, it was just the alcohol," we are driven back out to the airplane by the RCMP. It is part of the contract that the airline has with the Department of Justice that there is a cooler of beverages on the plane for the passengers, and this cooler contains primarily alcoholic beverages: small bottles of wine, cans of beer, and a bottle of expensive Scotch whisky. The judge and the lawyers and the clerk, upon boarding the airplane for the return trip, stop first at the cooler at the back of the plane and select their drink of choice. Many then consume alcohol on the way back. Upon arriving at the airport at home, these same people who were part of trying, convicting, and sentencing people for things committed while under the influence of alcohol, who heard all the devastating stories about the victims, about broken arms, missing teeth, stabbings, shootings, and beatings, and about people being run over by drunk drivers, well, they get in their cars and drive home.

These people, and many like them, have their own story about alcohol. In their story alcohol is a good thing. It is part of the fabric of their society. It is a tool for social bonding. It is medicine—medicine for the mind. It relieves stress. It helps them to relax. They never seem to be able to connect their own personal story about alcohol and themselves with the stories that they hear all day in court.

No, *niwâhkomakanak*, we can never expect the people who work in the justice system to solve our problem with alcohol. Sometimes, they are too numbed by alcohol themselves to ever be part of the solution.

Of course, it does us no good to point fingers. Pointing at *kiciwamanawak* judges and lawyers and saying,

"Look at how they behave," doesn't help us. We should pay attention to what they are doing only to recognize that they live in a different story. In their story, alcohol is not the great destroyer.

We cannot depend upon their law to solve any of our problems, because law is not rational. To solve a problem rationally, you first look at the problem, then you look at all the things to which the problem is connected. You ask, "How is this problem related to everything around it? How am I related to this problem?" After you have rigorously and honestly examined the problem and all its relatives, then you decide how to solve the problem, based upon everything that you know about yourself, the problem, and its relations.

But law doesn't work that way. In law there are two sides. Each side in the adversarial system decides which answer they want before they look at the problem. In criminal law the defence lawyer wants his or her client to not face a penalty and, ideally, to be found not guilty. The prosecutor wants a finding of guilt. The defence lawyer will look through the evidence and select all the things that show that the accused is not guilty. The prosecutor will look through the same pile of evidence and select all the things that prove guilt. Then, both the prosecutor and the defence lawyer will put the evidence they have selected before a judge to make a decision.

A judge is never given all the evidence. Both defence and prosecution deliberately leave out evidence that does not support their argument. The rules of disclosure require the prosecutor to give all the evidence to the defence. But there are no rules that say that the prosecutor has to tell the judge everything she knows. And, likewise, the defence has no obligation other than to defend her client. The judge then decides, based only upon what information is given to him. Even then, there is evidence that is not looked at because the law says that there is some evidence that a judge cannot consider.

The answer to the problem, which the judge then comes up with, is a legal answer. He will take the limited evidence put before him and then look at the law. He will look at the Criminal Code of Canada, he will look at the common law and read Supreme Court decisions, and he will look at the Charter of Rights and Freedoms. All these areas of law will tell him the rules he has to follow to come to a decision. The answer he comes up with might be correct in law, but it rarely ever solves the problem.

The Charter of Rights and Freedoms and the Criminal Code of Canada are both stories about how the law is supposed to work. These stories tell of strict rules of interpretation and fundamental rights and the procedure that is to be followed by judges and lawyers. The Supreme Court of Canada writes stories about each case it hears. Each decision is written as a parable that tells judges and lawyers how to act when they come across a story like the one the Supreme Court just heard.

Witnesses and accused persons each come to court with a story, the story of their lives, their relatives, their communities, and about what happened that brings them to court. They are asked questions when they give their evidence, but the questions asked by the lawyers are designed to get only the answer the lawyers want and nothing more. A judge will often tell a witness to not talk about something because it is not relevant, even if it is clearly part of the story that witness has to tell. What the judge means is that within the rules of law, the entire problem cannot be examined. Law cannot look at the problem and all its relations. Law can look only at legal things.

The problem of alcohol cannot be examined by the courts because the fact that alcohol is responsible for half the deaths in this territory is not a legal problem. There is no law against this sort of genocide. The law can look only at who was driving the car when it ran over the child, and whether the police followed the strict rules about arresting the driver, and whether the driver was told he had a right to a lawyer, and whether the police can prove the driver was drunk at the time.

The story about how the child came to be playing on the street, the story of the grief of the parents, the story of the other children that child played with and went to school with, the story of the community and of the funeral, the story of that child's dreams and aspirations, the story of the bootlegger who brought the bottle to the community and sold it to the driver, the story of the bootlegger's family, the story of the driver's family, the story about how this family now feels that they are not liked by that other family—none of these stories will be told to the judge.

The law story deliberately blinds the court. It's as though they can look at the problem only through pin-holes, look only at that tiny portion of the problem that the lawyers want looked at and that the law allows.

Law can never solve our problem with alcohol in our communities and the devastation it causes, because law is not rational. It refuses to look at the whole of the problem, even though alcohol and its aftermath are the primary matters that the courts deal with every day, all day long. In its deliberate blindness, law is actually quite insane.

8. FOUR MODELS

The law in this country can insist only that all adults have the human right to drink alcohol if they wish. That is a human rights story. But the Law Enforcement Model cannot answer to or help or solve this story—one of every two people in our communities dies an alcohol-related death.

9. THE TRICKSTER IN THE STORY

We do not know anything for certain. Everything we think we know comes from the stories we have been told or the stories that we tell to ourselves. We have been told stories in one form or another ever since we first learned language.

When I first came into this world, someone put a nipple in my mouth and I tasted warm milk. At the same time I heard sounds. My mind put these two things together—the taste of warm milk and a particular sound—and in my mind they became related. That is the beginning of how I learned language. I matched up the sounds I heard with what I was experiencing. At first I didn't know very much, but as I grew, so did my understanding. With every new experience my understanding grew. I looked at a new experience and figured out what it meant, based on what I thought I already knew. I began to put together the story of who I was and to whom I was related.

Later, I went to school and learned more stories. Every time I heard a new story, I figured out what it meant, based upon the body of knowledge that was already in my mind. Through grade school, then high school, into the workforce, then university, raising a family, participating in society, my story grew, and each time it grew, the new growth was based upon the previous understanding. I interpret everything I experience based upon what I already think I know, going all the way back to that first taste of warm milk in my mouth and the sounds my mother made.

If, anywhere along the way, I misinterpreted something, everything that followed would be tainted, because everything I think I know is based upon previous things I thought I knew. If there was a mistake anywhere along the way, then everything I think I know might be wrong.

I am the same as you, *niwâhkomakanak*. We are humans. We make mistakes. That is what makes us human. Our traditional stories and teachings remind us that each person has their own understanding of their place in the universe and it is not for us to tell them any differently, because we cannot know any better than they do. All that we can possibly have is our own interpretation, based upon our personal life experiences, and everyone's will be different. None of us can claim that our interpretation is the correct one.

In our traditional society, each person is allowed to experience being a spirit in a physical body and to grow their own understanding of what that means. We don't tell each other how to be. Everyone is free to go up on a high hill or some other isolated place to fast and pray and develop their understanding. We develop our understanding through other ceremonies as well, such as the Sundance and the Sweat Lodge. We might perform these ceremonies with others, but the understanding that we receive is uniquely our own. The dreams and the visions we sometimes receive are given to us to help us along our path.

When *kiciwamanawak* came here, they had different stories. In their stories they believed in absolute truths. If someone knew an absolute truth, they could tell everyone else in their society to follow that absolute truth. They believed that their king or queen had received, from God, the divine right to rule—that God had given the king or queen the heavenly right and power to have dominion over the people.

For about the first hundred years of this country, it was known as the Dominion of Canada. The original constitution of Canada refers to this country as a "dominion." That idea that the monarch was granted dominion over the people was slow to die. The people of Canada didn't really get away from using the term *dominion* until 1982, when the country here repatriated the constitution.

And so you see, *kiciwamanawak* stories change over time. They no longer believe that their queen has an absolute right to rule because she inherited the divine right from God. But the new story that has taken its place is presented again as an absolute truth. The constitution of Canada has taken the place of the queen, and the new story says that the constitution is the supreme law of Canada.

The belief in absolutes is one of the main differences between how we traditionally understood the universe and our place and our role in it, compared with this new way of being that *kiciwamanawak* brought here. In our old stories, the main character was usually the trickster. He created us, he created this land we call Turtle Island, and everything he touched had a way of turning itself upside down. We call the trickster Wîsahkicâhk. Our cousins the Anishinaabe call him Nanabush and our other cousins the Blackfoot call him Napi, but the stories of Nanabush, Napi, and Wîsahkicâhk are all the same.

In our stories nothing is ever presented as rigid and absolute. A fundamentalist is someone who takes a traditional story, like the Bible story or the Quran story, and says this story is true, right down to every single word, and we must abide by every word. It would be very difficult to become a Cree fundamentalist, because the person who tried to abide by every word would end up behaving like a clown, like Wîsahkicâhk, who often behaves foolishly.

Now we live in a world where things are taught and presented as though they are absolutely true and that there is no other way of knowing. Science is presented as though it were the last word on any subject. Economics are not to be argued with. Government might be full of tricksters, but the laws that they create and that are upheld by the courts are always absolute laws. We are told that there is one right way of knowing, that we have to think logically, and if we don't know the right way, then we should ask the experts in law, in economics, in science, and they will tell us.

niwâhkomakanak, there is a problem with these stories. They are absolutely true only for a short period of time and then they change, and a new story is told as though it was always the absolute truth.[36] In the science story, the world used to be flat and was the centre of the universe, and the sun and moon and stars circled the earth on fixed tracks. The story changed, and in the new story, the earth became round. Then it changed again, and now the science story says that the earth is a small planet circling an ordinary star on the edge of an average galaxy, lost in a universe that might be infinitely large.

The science story of how we came to be here was once closely tied to the Bible story of a Garden of Eden.[37] Then it changed and, over the course of many changes, it is now presented as the "big bang" story: that the universe started with a single dot that exploded and is still exploding, and all the things that are now in the entire universe used to be in that single dot.

Most scientists still believe this story and would not argue against it, but some are beginning to disagree. The big bang story is slowly coming apart, and we can expect that soon another story will take its place. And we can expect that another story will replace that story and another story will replace that story and on and on and on. It seems that no matter what story they come up with, the trickster always has a hand in it and twists it. Maybe someday they will recognize that there are no absolute stories—that the Creator is a trickster.

Maybe someday, but not today. Today we live in a world where experts speak as though they know what is best, that there is one, single truth for everyone. Most of our old stories that explained the world as relationships, as flow and change, have been lost. Those stories were laughed at; they were called silly and simple. The story that Wîsahkicâhk created Turtle Island from a tiny handful of dirt that Muskrat brought to the surface during the Great Flood was considered impossible. But now, scientists looking at fractals are recognizing that the universe might be made out of a single, tiny thing that repeats itself over and over and over again, and that everything is contained in the one, like the grains of earth that Wîsahkicâhk blew on, and the grains repeated themselves over and over again with each breath until Turtle Island was large enough.

It's not that their stories are not true, or that our stories are true; it's that no story is absolutely true. We take from traditional stories and from science and technology that which we can use to make our lives better today. No one knows better than anyone else how to live. All they have is the story that they were told, and the story is going to change tomorrow. So you can take only all that you know today, all that is your story, and live as best you can by it. But know too that the story will then change, and, as it does, you will know more and you will then be able to change and become better. You will take the best of each story and grow and do better.

Thinking is like a walk in the forest. The first time through, it's difficult, you break branches out of the way, your feet push down on the moss. The more often you walk through the same area, the easier it becomes. Eventually you have a trail to follow, a trail of your own making. Thinking works the same way. The first time you are thinking about something new, it's difficult. The more often you think about the same thing, the easier it becomes. Your brain creates networks that allow you to think the same thought over and over again. It follows the path you created. Pretty soon it seems like there is no other way of walking, or of thinking.

The alcohol story has been repeated so many times, we have thought about it in the same way so many times, that now for many of us it seems natural, normal, and even necessary. How many times have you heard that "we will never get rid of alcohol"? It has become such a powerful story that many cannot imagine a world without it.

Yet, a recent study has shown that 35 per cent of Aboriginal people in Canada are completely abstinent.[38] One out of three Aboriginal people does not use alcohol at all. When we think about alcohol, we can think in new ways. We can think about those of us who walk in a sober way, people who create their own paths and have freed their minds from the alcohol story.

10. BEING FRANK: EXPOSING THE PROBLEM

The alcohol problem connects to every part of our communities, including health, education, crime, violence, police, children, employment, food, leadership, shelter, suicide, hope, relations, despair, welfare, displacement, housing, parenting, environment, and religion. It doesn't matter where we start looking at the problem, because to solve it rationally we must look at it from all directions. A straight-line way of thinking (A+B=C) will not work. Alcohol touches every part of our lives, whether we drink or not. We cannot separate ourselves from the problem. It touches us, no matter what we do. Even if we don't drink, we have relatives who do, relatives who are suffering. Even if we don't drink, we live in communities that are being destroyed by alcohol.

Alcohol causes people to be displaced; they move to get away from alcohol and the violence and despair caused by alcohol. Even if they are living sober lives away from the community, it is alcohol that caused them to leave. Whether we drink or not, whether we live in the community or move away, alcohol touches us on several levels. Any solution will have to deal with all these ways that alcohol hurts us.

It doesn't matter where we start looking at the problem, so let's start with Creation. We have a story about how the Creator gave us our original instructions, that he put that message inside of us. Things like morals, ethics, kindness, and empathy were given to us as gifts to carry. Another way of seeing it is that our morals and ethics were written in our DNA. We are coded to behave in a good way. It doesn't matter which story we follow, whether it is our own stories about Creation, or the Christian story, or the science story—they all point to the idea that we carry our goodness within ourselves.

We have moral codes for a reason. We have ethics and inhibitions that help us live together. We don't normally shout and yell and raise hell, because we know it disrupts our communities and our families. Normally we behave as good people, living together with other good people. We have internal rules and taboos that help us to behave. Our inhibitions are there for a reason.

Then we drink alcohol. Alcohol's first symptom is to attack that part of the brain that inhibits our behaviour.[39] That feeling of dis-inhibition is what we are looking for when we go drinking. This is the feeling that we can sing, we can laugh more easily, we can dance, and we can say what we really think. It's a feeling of freedom. The fear that the drinker is being watched or others might disapprove is dissolved by alcohol with the first drink. Alcohol attacks those things that make us good, responsible people; we begin to speak louder and interrupt each other. If we now feel that we can speak freely, it's because we now often speak rudely.

10. BEING FRANK: EXPOSING THE PROBLEM

It's also this feeling of dis-inhibition that makes us feel relaxed. We don't worry about what others might think. That little voice in our head that tells us to behave is silent. Our moral code doesn't wrap itself around us as tightly. All those things that make us good people, that help us to live together as a community and as families, our ethics, all the social constraints, all the rules of proper behaviour begin to melt away with the first drink. With that melting away we feel relaxed; we can now speak, sing, laugh, dance, flirt, let go. Alcohol doesn't dissolve stress. It dissolves the rules and the feeling of responsibility that create the stress.

As we begin to feel relaxed, as our code of conduct disappears, we do things that we normally would not do. We have an affair; we cheat on our partners. Then we have to face the results when our partners find out. We lose our families; we lose friends along with our partners. Our children suffer.

Or we spend money that we know is needed for something else. Even though when we are sober, we love our children and want the best for them, when we're drinking, it's easy to buy another bottle with money that we know should be used to buy clothing or food or school supplies.

The more we drink, the weaker our moral code becomes. As I've told you, several times a day while I was in court, I'd hear someone say, "When he's sober, he's a good guy, it was just the alcohol." Someone drank until his or her normal code of behaviour dissolved and they committed an atrocity. How else do you explain a man beating up his mother? His children? How do you explain the violence against women? Against Elders?

In my experience as a Crown prosecutor in the provincial court system, most of the charges for violence were laid against men for beating up their partners. It is a charge that is prosecuted, often several times a day, in every provincial court in our territory. Over and over, these victims of domestic violence have told me that they wanted to drop the charges. They said, "When he's sober, he's a good guy. It was just the alcohol."

I've heard that phrase—"when he's sober, he's a good guy"—so many times that it is etched on my brain. Maybe she's just making excuses for him. Maybe she's trapped in a cycle of violence and dependence. Maybe she is merely the product of those sociological factors we have read about, but, when you hear the same thing repeated several times a day, over the course of years, you begin to believe what the women are telling you.

Women are also behaving badly because of drinking alcohol. More and more, the violence that we hear about in court has been caused by women. Traditionally, women are the caregivers in our communities, in our families. A woman is the first person a child looks up to.

A woman came up to me the other day to complain about police behaviour. She had been arrested in her own home and taken out to the police vehicle, wearing no pants. She thought the police had treated her with disrespect because they let the community see her nakedness, and she was extremely embarrassed. It turned out that it was her husband who phoned the police because she was drunk and trying to fight. She was smashing things, throwing a tantrum, angry, yelling and swearing and trying to hit people.

The husband had quit drinking a few months earlier and was trying to maintain a sober household. He couldn't imagine any way to solve the situation other than by phoning the police to arrest his wife, as she was completely out of control. She had drunk so much that her normal control, her dignity and respect, had dissolved, and she had melted down into a state of anger and violence.

And yet this is a woman who values her position in the community. She is a hard-working caregiver and homemaker, a mother and a grandmother. She had put up with a lot of abuse from her husband for years when he was drinking and had often phoned the police when he had mistreated her and the children. She was normally a strong woman who was able to keep going, keep holding her head up, who took pride in her strength of character. But when she drank, all that strength disappeared and all the past injustices that she had endured came rushing to the surface, and she did not have her normal ability to control herself.

None of this is easy to write, to speak of. We want to hide it away. But if we are going to start to try solving the problem of how alcohol is ruining us, we need to speak frankly, put it out into the light of day so we can see it, take an honest, hard look at it.

Why aren't we doing this? Given all we know about alcohol, its harm to the health of our bodies, our families, our communities, why aren't we doing more—something—about it?

11. COSTS OF THE ALCOHOL STORY

The government of Saskatchewan levies a tax on the alcohol sold in the province. A common explanation for why the government does not do anything about the damage caused by alcohol is that the government would have to give up this revenue. The Liquor Consumption Tax rate is 10 per cent. According to a government website,[40] the government of this province received about $88 million in revenue from the sale of alcohol in 2015. The provincial government spent $190,288,000 in 2014–15 on policing.[41] In talking to police officers, I am told that they spend about 75 per cent of their time taking care of intoxicated people.[42] Seventy-five per cent of $190 million equals $142 million. The money the government receives from the sale of alcohol does not come close to paying the cost of policing the inebriated. There's one cost to think about.

Next, the provincial government spends over $5 billion annually on health care.[43] We know that alcohol causes heart disease; it also causes several forms of cancer. Alcohol is involved in most injuries, including car and snowmobile accidents, drowning, stabbing, shooting, beating, suicide, house fires, and freezing. Alcohol consumption causes brain damage (dementia and difficulties with coordination and motor control), depression, increased risk of suicide, increased risk of high blood pressure, increased risk of stroke, liver damage, stomach ulcers, blood-vessel disorders, impotency in men, menstrual irregularities in women, addiction, and death.

The tax the government receives from the sale of alcohol is less than 2 per cent of the annual cost of health care.

There are no statistics about the amount of money spent on health care for treating alcoholics and the inebriated. It seems no one wants to know. When I first started thinking about alcohol and its costs, I found a forensic anthropologist. This was a man who had the tools and expertise to determine the total costs. I phoned him to set up a meeting and when we met at Tim Hortons, I explained to him in detail what I hoped he would do. I told him I would help to publish his findings and offered to co-author any report. I offered to assist in any way that I could, but please would he do the math, would he come up with the numbers? I wanted to find out many things. How many deaths were the direct results of alcohol? What percentage of accidents? How many cancers? How many heart attacks? How many suicides? Could he determine how much shorter a child's life would be because the parents were drinking and not providing proper nourishment during the child's formative years? What is the cost to society for one child with Fetal Alcohol Spectrum Disorder (FASD) during that child's life due to the increased cost to education should he require a special needs tutor, the cost to social services because he would have problems getting employment, the increased cost to policing when he messed up, to corrections because the justice system has no alternatives but to send him to jail, and the increased cost to health care, including mental health?

Near the end of our two-hour meeting, I was nearly begging, but he continued to refuse to undertake this research. I couldn't understand why. Was it too difficult? Too time-consuming? But when we were leaving, standing outside in the parking lot, he admitted that he still liked to have a drink now and then.

Because I have been unable to obtain the precise numbers of what alcohol costs us as a society and what the statistics are for alcohol-related deaths, I have been forced to estimate, and my estimate remains at one-in-two. That is, *every second person in this Treaty 6 territory is going to die from an alcohol-related death, whether they drink or not.* And, I have come to believe that this estimate might be low. In one community I recently visited, where the population is about 1,800 people, I was told by a community member that in 2015 they had sixty-six deaths and sixty of them were because of alcohol.

niwâhkomakanak, we are the only people who know about what is going on in our territory. We know because we keep burying our relatives, we keep standing at those gravesides and saying goodbye. No one else is going to do anything about it. It's not their problem; it's ours. You and I have to find the solution.

12. EMPLOYMENT

In our communities, a lot of people do not have a job. There are many reasons for this. There are two main areas where a person can work in our territory. The first is in resource extraction. We can go to the mines and dig uranium out of the ground, or we can chop down the forest and haul it away. If we go mining, we have to leave our homes and live part-time in a camp. The average pay in the mines is usually just a little less than is paid in other industries in Canada. We have had to struggle over the last few decades to convince the mining companies to hire people from this territory, and now some jobs are available. We can work as cooks and cleaners, as labourers and equipment operators, and occasionally one of our people goes to university and becomes an engineer. The mines are comparable to any other industry in Canada with regard to safety and security.

The other resource-extraction employer in our territory is logging. There was a time when there were over a thousand of us in the logging camps. Mechanization has replaced most of the work, and now only a handful of us are still employed there.

Commercial fishing is also a form of resource extraction. We once had a fish-processing plant in nearly every community in our territory, and many of us made our living that way. With a change in government policy away from local fish co-operatives toward a national marketing strategy, the small processing plants have disappeared along with the employment they provided. We still fish commercially, but it doesn't pay as well as it once did.[44]

When I was young, almost everyone in this territory made their living by trapping. We all fondly remember a time when families went out to the trapline and stayed there for months at a time. And then we came to town with our bundles of fur and sold them, and how good we felt, how proud we were. But then Greenpeace happened and fashions changed. The rich elite of America and Europe quit buying our fur, and we began to stay in town.

Resource extraction is a small employer compared with the service sector, the other main area for work. Most of the jobs in our territory are in government: schools, social services, health care, justice, policing, highways, etc. Most of our communities have a school that employs not only teachers, but also tutors, special-needs workers, cleaners, and security. The industry related to health care is a big employer beyond doctors and nurses; it employs people to clean and to cook and to drive and to keep records and maintain buildings. Likewise in justice and policing: there are more people employed than just lawyers, judges, and police officers. There are also clerks and cleaners.

And so there is some work in our communities, but there is not enough to go around. We also have people who will not work because they are too entangled in alcohol to get themselves to work. The Victim Model explains addictions by saying that part of the problem is unemployment. People without jobs drink more. But I'm going to go through this again: we have to ask ourselves, Do people drink because they don't have a job, or do people not have a job because they drink?

niwâhkomakanak, imagine that we were able to solve the problem of alcohol. Imagine that someone went up on a hill and prayed and came back with a vision or a song that solved this alcohol problem. Imagine that we were able to change our story and in the new story we didn't have alcohol. Imagine what it would be like if everyone in our territory was suddenly sober.

If half of all deaths in our territory are alcohol-related, at least half of the people who work in health care would be laid off: half of the doctors, half of the nurses, half of the cooks and cleaners.

When he was in charge of F Division, Assistant Commissioner Russ Mirasty told me that in the North, a minimum of 75 per cent of a policeman's job was dealing with intoxicated people, especially so when dealing with violence. When I put this number to police officers I met in the North, they readily agreed and said that in their experience, it was probably higher. But let's use Russ Mirasty's minimal number of 75 per cent. In that case, 75 per cent of the police would be transferred out of our territory.

As I have said, in my experience, 95 per cent of the people who come before the provincial courts were intoxicated at the time they committed their offence. If we solve the problem of alcohol, then 95 per cent of the judges and lawyers would have nothing to do and would have to reinvent themselves. Most of the prison guards would not have a job. The probation officers and parole officers could stop writing reports.

There would also be layoffs at the schools. We wouldn't require special-needs tutors because there wouldn't be any FASD students.

There wouldn't be a shortage of mental-health workers; we wouldn't need as many psychologists and psychiatrists.

There would be massive layoffs in social services too. We wouldn't need child-protection workers. Parents would be sober and so could look after their own children. There would be no foster homes, no youth detention centres.

The liquor stores would close down and the bootleggers would have to find a new way to exploit their neighbours. The people who work in recycling wouldn't have as many bottles and cans.

What am I getting at? Well, I suggest that alcohol is the biggest single employer in our territory. If we were to get rid of alcohol altogether, then we would have to completely re-imagine how we are going to live. We would have to create a new story for ourselves.

Until then, however, the cost of alcohol touches every one of us. We all know someone, a family member, a friend, a co-worker, who is suffering from addiction, and we have all buried someone. But the cost of alcohol is also in everything around us.

Alcohol abuse adds costs to manufacturing through absenteeism, illness, insurance, and lower productivity.[45] The manufacturer passes those costs on to us. They are built into the price of the car or the television or the light bulb. Alcohol abuse costs are in the price we pay for our shoes and our underwear. We pay a subsidy when we buy a three-piece chicken dinner or a hamburger, because the restaurant owner makes up his lost revenue by charging us more.

Everything that we build—every hospital, every school, every highway—costs more because of lost productivity due to alcohol use and abuse. There is an added cost to engineering for our highways because they need to be made safer, due to drunk drivers. Emergency-room waiting times are directly proportional to alcohol use and abuse. If teachers are drinking, that affects the quality of our education and our children's education, whether we drink or not.

We've been saying for years that there is a housing shortage in our communities. Yet, when I talk to the people who work in housing on our First Nations reserves, they talk about repairing the damage to houses caused by alcohol: the kicked-in doors and broken windows, the house fires.

We seem to be caught in a cycle. We claim to drink because we have nothing to do, and in our drinking we create the misery, dysfunction, and violence that drive the greater part of our economy. Most of the infrastructure in our territory—the hospitals, police stations, the courts, and the jails—depend upon our continued suffering. If we refuse to suffer from alcohol, all those systems of control (the courts, police, and social services) will no longer have a purpose, and we can go back to living free, independent lives. And, maybe, if we are sober, we can imagine how to make our living from the land again.

13. THE STORY WE TELL OURSELVES

am the son of a trapper and commercial fisherman. I grew up in the story of trapping and fishing. In this story I would be self-sufficient, I would earn my living through hard, honest work, and I would be proud of myself. Everyone around me was in the same story. All the kids I knew at school were the children of trappers and fishers. The story was complete. It contained everything in my experience, and I didn't know any stories outside the story of myself, my parents, my friends, and my relatives.

Then a man in my community came home after serving in the armed forces. He had been to Egypt and Cyprus as a peacekeeper. I heard his stories and my story grew to include his story, and I was able to imagine joining the armed forces.

At the age of seventeen, I joined the Canadian navy. I became a sailor. My story changed again and I took into myself all the stories and songs from the maritime tradition. Sailors drank hard and raised hell. They sang raunchy songs and got into fights with sailors from other countries. Alcohol on board a Canadian ship was duty-free. I paid fifteen cents for an ounce of hard liquor from a bar on board the ship. If I wanted to mix the rum I bought from the bar with Coke, there was a pop machine. A can of pop cost thirty-five cents. Right beside the pop machine was a beer machine. Beer cost twenty-five cents. Anytime I wanted a beer, all I had to do was put a quarter into the slot and a can of beer would drop out of the bottom of the machine. The beer machine was available twenty-four hours a day.

Alcohol was almost free and readily available at any time. All the people I sailed with were drinkers. We lived the story of sailors, and alcohol was a large part of the story. It seemed that alcohol was the central theme of the sailor story.

Then I got out of the navy. All my older brothers were loggers or miners. I heard their stories about mining and logging so I was able to imagine being a logger or a miner. Alcohol was also part of these stories. People frequently brought a bottle or bottles with them to the mining and logging camps to drink after work. Coming back from the camps with a pocket full of money often resulted in a week-long drunk before going back to work again.

My story, the story I told myself, was the hard-working, hard-drinking, tough son-of-a-bitch sailor, miner, logger story. There were no inconsistencies in my story. It was the same story that I heard from all the other miners and loggers and sailors. I became the story that I told myself. I became the hard-working, hard-drinking, tough son-of-a-bitch I had told myself that I was. I convinced myself that this was the real me, that all I was doing was being myself, my natural and normal self.

Then I became a father and I had to change my story. I modified it. I became the hard-working provider and protector. My drinking slowed down because the pro-vider part of my new story replaced some of it. But drinking was still a significant part of my life, and I couldn't imagine my story without it. Alcohol had been in my story all my life.

Then my marriage broke down, probably because of the hard-working, tough son-of-a-bitch attitude that I carried, and I found myself standing alone. I decided to go to university and study law. My story changed again. Now I was the hard-working student, determined to jump through all the flaming hoops that students are put through at law school. I told myself a new story and believed the story I was telling myself. I was the intel-lectual equal of everyone there, including the profes-sors. To maintain this story I was telling myself, I had to reduce the amount of alcohol I drank. I couldn't make it through university and drink heavily at the same time.

But alcohol remained part of my story. When I had been in the navy I drank rum because that was a sail-or's drink. As a student, I drank only twelve-year-old Scotch. This was a high-class drink. This was the drink that professors and business people and lawyers and judges drank. I was going to be a lawyer, and single-malt, twelve-year-old whisky was part of the lawyer story. I convinced myself that it tasted wonderful and believed that I could tell the difference between the taste of cheap whisky and expensive whisky.

Everyone has their story. It's the story they grow up with and it's the story they grow as they experience new things. If alcohol was part of our parents' story and our grandparents' story, if it's part of the story of our com-munity, of our friends, or our partners, then it will likely become part of our own personal story. It will be the story we tell ourselves about ourselves.[46]

I heard a very young man in our community say that people who didn't drink weren't real Indians. He obviously believed the *kiciwamanawak* story that has been going around about us. He took it as a true story and believed it. To him, his very being, his heredity, his culture, and his place in the universe were entangled in the alcohol story. This young man obviously believed that to be a real Indian meant being a drunk Indian. He actually believed that those who did not drink were not really Indigenous, they were outside the culture; they were trying to be pretentious and should be shunned as outsiders or even traitors to the cause.

The story about Indians and alcohol has been around for a long time. Remember those stories I told in the beginning? Remember those accounts by the fur traders and what they said about us and the firewater? We have lived in *kiciwamanawak*'s story for generations, and despite seeing what alcohol and this story do to us, despite the funerals and hospital visits, despite seeing our relatives hauled off to jail, for some reason, we continue to believe the story and tell it to each other and to ourselves.[47]

This does not have to be our story. It never was ours. It was *kiciwamanawak*'s story at the start. And we have the power to end it.

14. THE STORY *KICIWAMANAWAK* TELL THEMSELVES

Alcohol is not just in our stories—the stories that *kiciwamanawak* first told about us and that some of us continue to tell and believe. You see, alcohol is also in *kiciwamanawak* stories, the stories they tell about themselves. However, it is told much differently: they are never "the lazy, drunk, white person" in their own stories of alcohol.

To many *kiciwamanawak*, alcohol is an everyday thing. It's a glass of wine with supper, or a beer or two while watching the game on television, or a glass of whiskey in the evening. To them, alcohol is natural, normal, and even necessary. In their story about alcohol, their social position determines the amount they spend on alcohol. The higher they are in their social and class structure, the more expensive the alcohol they must consume.

In their story, if a person does not drink, it is automatically assumed they do not drink because they have a religious reason, or, more often, it is assumed it's because they can't handle it.[48] Only alcoholics in their story do not drink. Healthy, normal people in that story often consume alcohol daily. Every significant event is marked by alcohol: birthdays, marriages, graduations, a sports team winning (or losing), and even death is saluted with a drink, a toast. To not drink in the *kiciwamanawak* story is to cut oneself off from important parts of the story. Their story and the alcohol story are so entangled that one becomes the other. The *kiciwamanawak* story becomes the alcohol story and the alcohol story becomes the *kiciwamanawak* story.

One of our relatives gets into trouble while drinking. He or she goes to court and is sentenced. The sentence is given to try to help the person with their problem with alcohol. The person is put on probation or given a conditional sentence. The conditions might be: report to a probation officer, reside at an approved residence, abide by a curfew from 11:00 P.M. until 7:00 A.M., refrain from the possession or consumption of alcohol, and attend addictions counselling and treatment.

Then our relative goes to see the probation officer. The probation officers I have met typically are young; they will have had some formal education and will have attended a training course or two as part of their job. Most of them, though, I know to be drinkers. The probation officers typically are not from our community and they have their own story about alcohol. To them, alcohol is part of their existence. They don't even really think about it—it's so much part of their daily life.

The probation officer's job is to supervise the person on probation and make sure that person does all the things that are in the probation order. Usually, the person is ordered to report to the probation officer once a week. The probation officer normally flies into the community along with the judge and lawyers and clerk. They set up a table at the back of the community hall where court is being held and interview people who have been ordered to report. They will interview thirty to forty people a day. The reporting usually takes only a few minutes.

The probation officer asks, "How's it going?"
"I'm doing good, not getting in any trouble."
"Have you been drinking?"
"No."
"Have you gone for counselling?"
"Not yet."
"If you don't, you're going to be in breach of your order. So you better get it done."
And the person leaves, saying, "Yeah, I'll make an appointment next week."

Probation officers come in two types. One is there to enforce the probation order and file a breach-of-probation charge if the person doesn't comply with all the conditions. The other type of probation officer is there to help the person get through the probation period without breaching. Regardless of the type of probation officer, whether they are there to act as probation police or whether they genuinely want to help, if, in their story, alcohol is normal, natural, maybe even necessary to the enjoyment of their daily life, they will be limited in their ability to effect change in the person reporting.

I've frequently heard judges lecture people about drinking when they are sentencing: "You really have to get a handle on your drinking. You know every time you drink you get in trouble. If you keep going like this, you are going to end up in jail and I know you don't want that." Then these same judges get on the plane, leaving the community with this advice, and yet, as I've said, they are pouring themselves a drink even before takeoff.

And so here's one of the problems, if we're being frank and getting to the root: the person who is being sentenced, standing in front of the judge in the court-room, or the person reporting to the probation officer at the back of the community hall, they know that the words spoken to them are not genuine, that the peo-ple speaking them don't practise them. They're empty words, without power. Hypocrisy—it comes through in the voice. You can hear it. The words are without mean-ing, they have no heart, no sincerity, no genuine feeling.

We cannot blame these judges and probation offi-cers for their empty words. They see that the problem is always alcohol. It's obvious. It repeats itself over and over every day in court, fifty, sixty, seventy times a day in docket court, and eight, nine, ten times on trial days. Two or three times a month the court party flies into these communities, and the trial days and the docket days become a long string of stories of violence and abuse and damage: broken windows and kicked-down doors, black eyes and broken teeth and knife wounds and skulls cracked by whisky bottles, until everyone involved just becomes numb and all they can do is repeat the obvious: "You have to quit drinking."

But the judges and probation officers who are numbed by the repetition are themselves drinkers, who live a story where alcohol is normal, natural, and necessary, and so they are simply incapable of putting any real meaning into their words. Their story, the story *kiciwamanawak* tell themselves about alcohol, cannot help us.

15. ADDICTIONS

The problem is not addictions. Even if we had a rehab centre in each of our communities and each one was fully staffed with well-trained professionals, we would still have a problem with alcohol. The problem is primarily drinking, not addictions.[49] I see a multitude of young people before the courts on charges and often the charges allege serious violence. What happened was that they were angry. They were angry because of the conditions in which they live. They were angry because of the story they tell themselves, and so they went drinking. Drinking then reduced their ability to control themselves and they lashed out, sometimes with fatal consequences.

Or they were simply on a party, out to have a good time, but with alcohol, and so things went badly. They were driving and someone got run over, or the car rolled and now they are charged with impaired driving causing bodily harm. Or, they did something else that was equally stupid, not because they are addicted to alcohol, but simply because they were drinking alcohol that one time.

15. ADDICTIONS

A young woman with no criminal record, who hadn't got into any trouble before, went out drinking with her girlfriends. Then they went to a house where they thought a party was happening. They were asked to leave. An argument broke out. Some fists were used. She hit a man and knocked him down, then hit him again to keep him down. She bragged on Facebook that she had knocked him out and laughed about it until she heard that she had killed him. Her two punches had caused a massive brain bleed and he died without ever regaining consciousness. And this was a woman who rarely drank.

The young people we see again and again in court are rarely alcoholics. They haven't drunk long enough, or hard enough, to become addicted. They are in court because in the story they have been telling themselves, alcohol is fun, or it's medicine, or it's simply part of their idea as to what Indigenous people are supposed to do to be truly Indigenous.

In fact, those who are alcoholics, who are going to drink themselves to death, are not in court very often, and when they are, they are usually there as victims. The ones who are completely addicted to alcohol tend not to hurt others. They are fully consumed with finding the resources to obtain more alcohol and don't have the time or the energy to get into trouble. They are picking cans or begging, and when they get enough for a bottle of cheap alcohol, they go off by themselves somewhere to consume it where no one will take it away from them.

I have gone out and interviewed people such as this in my community; they are known as the Muskeg Drinking Club. Before 1960 it was illegal for an Aboriginal person to purchase alcohol, and it was prohibited on the reserves. People would go to town and, if they managed to get a bottle, they would go out in the muskeg to drink it because they couldn't take it back to the reserve. It was a safe place to drink in peace and the police wouldn't bother them. Over the decades, the practice has continued as the old-timers die off and are replaced by younger members. Today they hang around panhandling or in other ways finding enough money so that they can chip in for a bottle. They take the bottle and go out into the muskeg to share it. The bottle is usually a very cheap red wine with an alcohol content of 20 per cent. It's a very inexpensive drunk. In my conversations with them, many have told me that they know the alcohol is killing them, that they know if they keep drinking, they are going to die from it. They told me stories of all the ones who weren't there anymore, about my friend who fell down the steps at the post office and hit his head, about the guy who was found drowned, the ones in the hospital who aren't likely to make it, the woman who came out in the middle of the night and no one was there and they found her frozen body the next morning, and they pass the bottle around.

I ask, "Why do you keep drinking?"

And they answer, "I've tried to quit but I can't, and anyways, I'm not hurting anyone except myself."

And so, while addictions are real and the consequences are fatal, the number of addicts is remarkably low. Despite being highly visible in the community—standing around in front of the liquor store day in and day out until everyone in the community knows them often by name—the Muskeg Drinking Club has only a few dozen members. As I said at the start, then, the problem we've got here is not so much about addiction as it is about alcohol use in general.

16. THE LAND

All wealth comes from Earth. All our clothes, our houses, our cars, gas and oil, our televisions, our iPods: everything is provided by that old grandma. We take the oil out of her body and make it into plastic. We take the iron from her and make metal. We take the trees that grow on her and make paper and build our houses. The cotton in our shirts grew out of nutrients she provided. Absolutely everything humans have built has come from the raw materials we take from Earth. Nothing comes from outer space except sunlight; well, and the odd meteorite.

Everything that *kiciwamanawak* built in this country came from materials they obtained by being adopted by our ancestors. All their cities, their railroads and highways and pipelines, all come from Earth. *kiciwamanawak* obtained the right to be here and to share the earth with us when our ancestors adopted them. They have done well for themselves. Canada is a very wealthy country. But few Canadians understand where their wealth comes from: most believe it comes from something magical called the "economy."

niwâhkomakanak, we now live in two worlds. We have our traditional world and the new world of work and employment and massive resource extraction and manufacturing. Most people in that other world believe their way of being is natural and necessary, that there could be no other way of being. In the economy story, everything depends upon how well the stock markets are doing. We have uranium mines in our territory and some of our people work there. The mines hire more people when the price of uranium is high and lay them off when the market drops. No one really knows what makes the markets go up and down. It's magic.

The economy story has many turns and twists to it, even though the main plot is easy to grasp. It's a story that *kiciwamanawak* tell to themselves and to others as though it is a true story, and perhaps to them it is. Remember I told you about how their stories are always put forward as absolute truths? But if you step back, step outside the story and look at it, this one too is simply another fiction.

Our stories, like *kiciwamanawak* stories, are also filled with magic, but our stories are rooted in the land and are about our place on the planet and how we came to be here and how we shared this planet with the plants and animals and with each other. People and animals could talk to each other then. And the earth and the four directions, not the economy, were what was filled with magic and power and what guided us.

I have been a writer for a long time now and know that the stories I create come from my place here on the land. Everything I write comes from here. Even as I sit and write these words, looking out my window at the forest, looking at the logs that make my cabin walls, looking at the grass and the river, I am filled with a sense of place. This is not just where I am. This is who I am. I am a child of the earth.

Alex Whiteplume from South Dakota once explained my relationship to the land. He said that long ago, when my ancestors died, their bodies were wrapped in a robe and placed on a scaffold toward the sky. The birds came and ate some of the body, and eventually the scaffold fell and the rest of the body came back to the earth. The worms ate the body then and took it into the ground. The grass roots reached down into the earth and took up my ancestor's atoms. The deer and moose and buffalo came and ate the grass. We killed and ate the moose and deer and buffalo, and in that way we took our ancestors' atoms into ourselves. My ancestors' atoms are in the earth and in me and in the birds and in all living things around me. I am part of the cycle of Earth and life and scaffold and sky and Earth again. I am part of the land and the land is part of me.

We live in two worlds: our traditional world and the new world economy. When we try to live in two worlds, in two separate stories, sometimes things can become confusing. In one world we are expected to go to school, graduate, get a job, raise a family, be successful, retire, and die. In the other world we get our education through living and fully experiencing our time on this planet, on this land.

So what does all this have to do with alcohol? Has my story gone astray? Not at all. Because let me now tell you the story about my uncle Johnny. He was a trapper and lived in a cabin on his trapline by himself. The cabin was about two kilometres' walk out to the main road, and sometimes when he became lonely he would walk out to the road and sit on a chair he had there. He just sat and waited, and when a vehicle came by and stopped, he would have a visit. I frequently drove that road on my way to town and back, and several times Johnny would come along for a ride to town, not because he needed anything, just for the visit.

He liked to laugh and he liked to tease and sometimes when he had money he liked to go to town and drink with his friends. He'd stay in town a few days, drinking and visiting and laughing, buy some supplies, and go back to the trapline to dry out. It became a pattern with him: go into town, go on a binge, then go back to the cabin to sober up.

One winter, one of those nasty winters when the snow was extremely deep, Johnny got stuck in town and had to stay around for longer than he usually stayed. The path back to his cabin was too difficult for him to walk. He was getting older and had injured one of his feet. Of course, because he was a trapper, he had nothing to do in town except drink, and so he drank. Without being able to go home and sober up and dry out, he drank steadily. His health wasn't good to begin with, and with constant drinking and not eating properly, it quickly became worse. The sicker he became, the more he drank, somehow thinking alcohol was medicine.

One day, staying at a friend's house, he phoned for a taxi. He wanted to go to the liquor store. The taxi driver was married to one of Johnny's nieces and knew Johnny quite well. The taxi driver saw the condition Johnny was in and agreed to take him to the liquor store only if Johnny agreed to go the hospital first to get checked over.

This was about noon. Within four hours of checking in at the hospital, Johnny died. All his internal organs had shut down. He had drunk himself to death. We buried him, said our goodbyes, tried to remember the good things in his life. Someone put flowers at the chair out by the highway, where we had so often seen him sitting, waiting for someone to come by and visit.

When Johnny was on the land, when he was in a familiar story, he did well. He lived a sober life and a good one. When Johnny went to town, to a story that didn't include him or fit him, he did the one thing the modern world allows old Indigenous trappers like Johnny to do: he drank. There are several like Johnny around: people living on the land and doing well and going to town only because they are lonely. In town they find themselves in a different world, unable to fit in and cut off from the land, and so they drink.

Quite often we come across someone in our communities who is on a binge, someone who started drinking and isn't stopping. They get themselves in trouble with the police—maybe they break a window or assault someone—and are released on an undertaking that includes a condition that they refrain from the possession and consumption of alcohol. A few days or a week later, the person is again found by the police and they're still drinking. The police charge them with breaching their conditions and release the person again. The pattern continues: breach by drinking, arrest, release. Then the police get tired of arresting the same person over and over again, and this time they keep him in custody, and he comes before the court to decide whether to keep him in jail or release him again on new bail conditions. A bail hearing is held and the Crown argues why the person should be kept in custody. The community doesn't want intoxicated people wandering around, getting in trouble, the police don't want to deal with the same person over and over again, and the accused person can't seem to sober up on their own, and if they keep drinking there is a likelihood that they are going to hurt themselves or someone else.

What to do?

Well, when I was a defence attorney, I frequently argued that my client in this situation should be released from jail to go back to the trapline—that he wouldn't be any trouble out there. Now, as a Crown prosecutor, I readily agree that an accused person can be released on bail if he plans to go to the trapline. But there aren't a lot of our people anymore who have a trapline. We now live in communities and the land is mostly empty of people. We have been disconnected from the land, taken from it, moved into this other world. In this other world, the only option then becomes jail.

When our ancestors negotiated Treaty 6, they sat on the ground. The Treaty commissioner sat on a chair. Our ancestors knew they occupied a position of strength. They were in direct contact with their mother, Earth, and her strength flowed through them. They used this advantage to press for a ban on alcohol. That understanding that Earth is our mother, that she can help us, that she is a source of strength and power, has been largely forgotten.

Some of us still have traplines. I frequently meet people who go to the trapline, not to trap, but just to be. They go to get away from all the noise and confusion of community living. They go to get away from the drunks. Maybe they go to a little cabin by a lake, a place where there are good memories—memories of Grandma and Grandpa and of laughter and wild food, memories of happy childhoods. They go back to the trapline to heal, to refill their spirits, to eat healthy food, to catch a fish from the lake or to set rabbit snares, or shoot a duck or a goose.

There is no money in trapping anymore. It is almost a shame to kill a beaver and sell the pelt for $20. You have to kill a lot of beaver to pay for the gas and the snowmobile to go get them. Most of us who are still trapping are not doing it for the money. We do it so that we can have a cabin, so that we have a place to go, a place to pick berries and mushrooms and medicines, a place away, a place where we feel connected to the forest, to the lakes and rivers, to the land, to *mithosin kitaskinâw*.

In town, away from the land, our youth get in trouble with the law. They commit mischief, they break into the school and vandalize it, they wander around in packs at night, looking for something exciting to do, and they steal a car and smash it up. They find a bottle and pass it around, and someone gets hurt. Then they come to court to answer for their mischief. They tell the judge, "There's nothing to do in this town. There are no recreational facilities." I come out of the court and look around at the welcoming forest that surrounds the town, at the lake inviting someone, anyone, to come and paddle across it, maybe even have a race if you're looking for excitement. I see fish jumping, wondering where the hooks are, where our people went.

I ask myself why, why, with this beauty all around, the spectacular landscape, raw nature in abundance, why would anyone believe they had nothing to do? Why would anyone want to play in a playground even if there was one, on swings and teeter-totters and jungle gyms, when there were so many trees to climb and rocks to fall off of and creeks to jump across? Every one of our communities has a lake to swim in and, when it freezes, that becomes a skating rink. We have a problem with stray dogs—dogs that could pull a sleigh loaded with children, laughing and falling off, getting their faces covered in snow, to laugh even louder and run to catch back up to the sleigh.

Where did this idea come from that there is nothing to do? What story are we telling our children? Are we telling them that the only things worth doing are the things that are in a story that doesn't fit here? Our children will grow up in the story that we create for them. If we don't tell them the trapline story, the hunting and fishing and trapping and gathering story, if the only story they see is the alcohol and violence story, they will live the alcohol and violence story.

Our land is mostly empty. It seems the only people out here are operators of mechanical harvesters, cutting down the forest and hauling it away. The government is supposed to consult with us before they do anything that infringes upon our rights as Aboriginal peoples. A logging company wants to clear-cut the forest in our traditional territory. The government sends a letter to the First Nation. Our leaders, our administrators, are so busy dealing with all the problems in the community caused by alcohol that they don't have the time or the extra resources to sit down with government and engage in thorough consultations. The letter from the government goes unanswered, and the logging company clear-cuts another trapline. And when the trapper complains, when he yells at government and says, "You never asked me before you cut all the trees on my trapline and now my cabin isn't in the forest anymore, it's out in the middle of a clear-cut," the government answers, "We sent a letter to your First Nation and offered to consult."

Our chiefs and councillors and administrators are too busy dealing with health and education and social services and the perpetual housing shortage and the water and sewers, trying to solve the violence against women, against Elders, and the child abuse and neglect. They don't look outside the community at what is happening in our traditional territory. And because there are very few of us left on the land, there are no eyes or ears to see and hear what is happening. While we close ourselves in our communities, while we look inward at all the turmoil and struggle to maintain the infrastructure and ourselves, the land is being destroyed.

17. IT'S ALL ONLY A STORY

Kayâs, Wîsahkicâhk came up to a lake filled with ducks and geese and loons and all sorts of delicious birds. He thought, Now, how am I going to trick those silly birds into being my lunch? He picked a whole bunch of reeds and made them into a bundle and went walking really quickly by the lake, acting like he had a great purpose with that bundle of reeds on his back.

The birds saw Wîsahkicâhk walking past and yelled out to him, "Wîsahkicâhk, nistîs, where are you going?"

Wîsahkicâhk acted like he didn't hear them and kept walking, looking straight ahead as though he was doing something very important.

Again the birds yelled at him, even louder. "Wîsahkicâhk, nistîs, where are you going? What are you doing?"

Wîsahkicâhk stopped. He said, "Oh, I'm sorry, nisimisak, I didn't hear you. I am on my way to see the Creator to bring him these Shut-Eye Dances he asked for."

"What are Shut-Eye Dances?" the birds asked.

"Oh, it's not for you. It's for the Creator."

"Come on, Wîsahkicâhk, tell us. We want to know about Shut-Eye Dances too."

"Alright then," he said. "I guess the Creator won't mind if I'm a little bit late. I'll show you."

So he went up on a nearby hill and built a little round lodge out of those reeds he had in his bundle, and he left a little door. He invited the birds to come in the little round lodge and he told them, "I am going to sit here beside the door with this drum and sing a song. You guys dance around and around in a circle with your eyes closed and that is Shut-Eye Dances."

Then he started hitting that drum and singing a song. That song was so sad that even Wîsahkicâhk started to feel like he was going to cry. And all the birds closed their eyes and danced around and around in a circle.

When a bird came close to Wîsahkicâhk, he grabbed it, wrung its neck, and threw it out the door behind him. He kept going like that, singing his sad song, beating the drum, and wringing birds' necks.

But one bird didn't trust Wîsahkicâhk. It was Loon. Loon started to dance but then decided to open one eye and he saw what Wîsahkicâhk was doing and he yelled, "Get out of here, my brothers! Wîsahkicâhk is killing us!" And all the birds ran out the door. Loon was the last one to go out. Wîsahkicâhk was angry with Loon for telling on him and as Loon was leaving, Wîsahkicâhk kicked him in the back end. That's why Loon walks funny even to this day. And that is why Loon has red eyes, from opening them in Wîsahkicâhk's lodge.

niwâhkomakanak, is that what we are doing? Are we dancing around and around with our eyes closed while alcohol is killing us? Have we too been duped? Have we fallen for a trickster's story about how important alcohol is to us as a people? Have we fallen for the story that we can't do without it?

Everything is story. I am story. You are story. The universe is story. I've explained how I am story, how I am all the things that I tell myself. I was once a sailor and a logger and a miner and told myself those stories, and so I lived them. Everyone does the same thing. They make up a story about themselves and say, "This is the real me," and then they live that way.

When I was a kid growing up in the community of Molanosa, no one had electricity except for the people who owned the store. Every few months we would run a power line from the store, across the highway, and over the hill to the community hall, so that we could show a movie. One of the movies was *Tarzan of the Apes*. For months after seeing that story, all the kids climbed trees and bent them over, trying to go from one tree to another. We broke a lot of trees.

After the movie *Zorro*, we played at sword fighting for months with willow branches. It was very painful play. Willows hurt when you get whacked across the side of your head by a kid who is using a longer branch for his sword than you are using for your sword. By the time we finally got a John Wayne movie, the swords had become ridiculously long.

John Wayne, cowboys and Indians, was a welcome reprieve.

"BANG! BANG! You're dead."

"No, I'm not. You missed."

"I don't miss, I'm John Wayne."

I might have been seven or eight years old and my family had gone down the east side of Montreal Lake by boat to a place where my father had a trapper's cabin. Most of the adults had walked inland to see the cabin, simply because they had so rarely seen it in summer. I stayed on the beach with the other children, who were more interested in swimming than in walking through an overgrown trail. My aunt Annie stayed behind to supervise us. After most of the adults left, I asked Annie, "What are we going to do if the Indians come?"

I still remember the look she gave me. "We are the Indians," she said. "What language do you think your mother speaks when she is not speaking English?" In my young mind, in the story from the John Wayne movie, Indians had feathers in their hair and carried tomahawks and shrieked when cowboys shot them. I had no idea that my parents, my grandparents, the children I swam with, the children I climbed trees with and had sword fights with, were Indians.

We can live any story that we want. We can live a drama—many people do—or we can live a romance, or a tragedy, or a comedy, or a mystery, or a fantasy, or a fable, or a fairytale. We can decide which story we want to be in and tell it to ourselves. The only limit on our ability to choose our own story is the story into which we are born. We have all been raised within a particular story. When we recognize it as story, it loses its power. This is especially true of victim stories. All of what we refer to as 'society' is the story that we tell ourselves about ourselves.[50]

Modern scientists have learned a few things about the smallest pieces of matter. They have discovered that if they test light, it can be either a photon or a wave. What makes it either one depends upon what they are testing for. If they are looking for a photon, then the light will be a photon. If they are looking for a wave, then light will be a wave. What does this have to do with stories? Well, like us, light will be whatever story scientists choose to tell about it.

They recently did a similar experiment with atoms.[51] Atoms are much larger than light photons. But the experiment came to the same conclusion. It didn't matter which story they told about the atom before the test, the atom became the story they told. If the story was that the atom was solid matter, it became solid matter. If they told the story about the atom's being energy, the atom became energy. Science, in fact, has understood this for a long time; Einstein[52] famously said, "Reality is merely an illusion, albeit a very persistent one."

When we look out at the universe, when we stand outside on a dark night and look up at the stars, we are not necessarily seeing stars and galaxies and planets that still exist. Some of the stars we see are no longer there. They burned out long ago. The light travelling from those distant places took millions of years to reach us. So what we are seeing is not the star, but the history of it.[53] We see its story written in light.

A large portion of what we see doesn't exist. We make it up. If we actually saw things the way our eyes work, we would see two pictures, one from each eye, and each picture would have a huge, gaping hole in the middle, because we do not see through the optic nerve in the centre of our retina.[54] Each picture would be clearer toward the middle and fuzzy around the edges. Our brain merges the two images and fills in the hole in the centre of each of them. What we see is not really there. Our brain simply makes it up. Our vision is fiction. Our eyes tell us stories.

In fact, you and I and all other living things are made of stories—stories made out of the letters found in our DNA. The genetic molecules in DNA form a code of four letters: A, C, G, and T. With that four-letter code, a four-letter alphabet, we can write every living thing on the planet. With those four letters, we not only write our eye and hair colour, how tall or short we are, whether we are likely to be wide or thin, whether we are likely to get this disease or that disease, we also write what our personality is going to be like, whether we will be aggressive or timid. Our ethics might also be written in there. Our moral code might be written with those four letters.

Our relatives the Iroquois have a story about how the Creator put our original instructions inside each of us. Did the Creator write our original instructions in DNA?

Russian physicist Victor G. Gorshkov calculated the information flow through earth's biota.[55] He said that the amount of information flowing through all the plants and animals combined was so great that if we were to try to replicate that amount of information flow with a computer, the size of the computer would have to be the same size as all of the earth's biota combined, and all that would be achieved would be to replace a natural carbon-based system with a silicon-based system.

Some people in the scientific theoretical community have suggested that all matter might just be information, that the entire universe might be nothing more than information. At a quantum level it is very difficult to say whether an atom or a smaller particle is solid or not, whether it is real or whether it is energy. This planet, us, all living things on this planet, the solar system, and the entire universe might just be a very complex story.

The Christian story says, "In the beginning was the Word, and the Word was with God, and the Word was God."[56] The Word is very important in that tradition. Moreover, in the Christian story, Jesus used parables to teach. These are powerful and timeless stories that his followers use to make sense of the world. We have the same practice with our traditional stories. We use them to make sense of the world.

Canada too is just a story. It is a story that has continued for over a hundred years, and we continue to write it. The border between Canada and the United States is an imaginary line. We take the story of that line very seriously and guard it. But it doesn't exist in any real form. We just made it up. It's a story. But it could change. The constitution of Canada is written in several documents. We can change them too. The story of Canada can be rewritten. It is a very powerful story, and many people have gone to war and died because of that story, but it is a story that can change all the same.

What else is just story? Corporations. They are not real. We made them up. Cameco and Exxon do not exist in any real form. They have no body. They have no soul. They are merely documents—stories—filed with the Corporations Branch of the government. We made up the Corporations Act that sets out the rights and privileges of corporations. The Corporations Act can be changed at any time. Cameco and Exxon and all other corporations are stories that we tell ourselves.

17. IT'S ALL ONLY A STORY

The economy is a powerful story. We give human sacrifice to it. There are people in poor countries who must starve to death because the economy story says that even though we have too much food in this part of the world, if we gave any to them, we would destroy the economy. We used to believe in dragons and unicorns. Now we believe in market forces. The economy doesn't exist. It's something we made up, and we gave it power. Whoever is in power gets to decide what the economy story is. As Max Tegmark, the theoretical physicist who first studied economics, states:

> Alas, I soon grew disillusioned, concluding that economics was largely a form of intellectual prostitution where you got rewarded for saying what the powers that be wanted to hear. Whatever a politician wanted to do, he or she could find an economist as advisor who had argued for doing precisely that. Franklin D. Roosevelt wanted to increase government spending, so he listened to John Maynard Keynes, whereas Ronald Reagan wanted to decrease government spending, so he listened to Milton Friedman.[57]

Law is a story. There are two sources of Canadian law: the common law and statute law. The common law is made up of all the cases heard by the courts and written in decisions. This body of law goes back several hundred years. Each decision is a story about what happened in that particular case. There are now hundreds of thousands of these stories that judges and lawyers today read and rely upon to make decisions about what they are going to do in their particular cases. When these stories are put together, the common law becomes a multi-volume saga about authority.

Statute law is made up of all those laws that are passed by government and includes the Criminal Code of Canada, the Highway Traffic Act, and hundreds of other forms of legislation that determine how the environment is regulated or not regulated, how often an airplane has to be inspected, and whether or not we have to wear seat belts. Each piece of legislation is a story about how we are going to behave in a particular situation, and it is constantly being changed and modified. We continuously rewrite these stories.

Psychiatry is story. If you go to a psychiatrist, she has you lie on a couch and asks you to tell her the story of when you were a child. It's not the psychiatry that doctors your mind; it's you. You rearrange your thoughts, you put them in order, you make sense out of them, so that you can tell the story. That's what storytelling is. Storytelling is how we make sense out of our world.

As you can probably tell, what I'm getting at is this: stories are very powerful. In fact, stories are so powerful they can either heal or kill you. If I gave you a sugar pill and told you that it would cure whatever it was that you were ailing from, and you believed the story I told you about the sugar pill and you took the pill, there is a very good chance that your symptoms would go away. We have known about the placebo effect for a long time. There is also a nocebo effect. In this case, I give you the same sugar pill but I tell you that it is poison, and if you take the sugar pill and believe the story, there is a good chance that you will become very sick and possibly die.

Everything is story. I am story, you are story, the universe is story, and all these stories work together to create what we experience as reality. A story doesn't make sense by itself. It depends upon all the other stories that support it. This is what we call "context."

And though I've said that we decide what story we want to live in, we can live only in a story that makes sense in relation to all the stories around us. My story is a continuation of my parents' stories. It's shaped by my education, by my experiences, by the books I have read and the movies I have watched. I can be whatever story I can imagine, but my imagination is affected by all the stories that surround me.

What does all this have to do with alcohol?

Alcohol is just a story. It's a powerful story. It's a story that surrounds us. It's in the movies that we watch, it's in advertising, it's in the story that our friends tell us and our parents told us, or showed us. Alcohol is part of the accepted history of our people. The fur traders who first met us began the story of the Indian and alcohol, and that story was allowed to grow until it became the dominant story about us. Most of us have heard these stories about us all our lives. We don't want to hear them anymore. We want to be normal. And when we try to be normal, there's that alcohol story again.

The danger of the alcohol story is when we accept it as natural, normal, and necessary, when we use it as medicine to dissolve grief, or as a way to cope. The story needs to be taken apart and examined. How much of it is made up by the companies that sell alcohol? How much of the alcohol story is simply wrong? The danger of this story is not what *kiciwamanawak* might think about us. The danger is in whether or not we believe the 'drunken Indian' story and all the other stories about us and all the other stories about alcohol.

We don't want to be the birds in the Wîsahkicâhk story, doing the Shut-Eye Dance, do we? And even though it might be hard—for, as you recall, the legend says that Loon has red, painful eyes because he dis-obeyed and opened them in the Sacred Lodge—it would be better for us to see things that are painful—through a veil of tears, even—than not to see at all.

18. BANNING ALCOHOL

Everything is story. You are story. I am story. The universe is story. God is story. The earth is story, right down to its smallest parts. Everything we believe in and everything we think we know is story.

Alcohol is story too. It's about class and culture and religion. In chemistry it is known as "ethanol." Its chemical formula, which is a complete story in itself, is C_2H_6O, meaning it is made of two atoms of carbon + six atoms of hydrogen + one atom of oxygen. If we change one part of this chemical formula, take away any one of the atoms, be it a single carbon, hydrogen, or oxygen atom, the substance will no longer be alcohol.

If we change our story about alcohol, if we stop accepting it as natural, normal, and necessary, if we stop telling ourselves that alcohol is medicine, that it dissolves grief, maybe we won't have to stand at so many gravesides and mourn so many senseless deaths.

We know that banning alcohol does not work. That was tried during the Prohibition Era. Famously, from 1920 to 1933, the United States prohibited the sale, manufacture, and transportation of alcohol without ever prohibiting the consumption of alcohol. It was illegal to make, sell, or move alcohol, but a person could legally drink as much as they could get. We know the results. Canadians became rich by making and smuggling alcohol to dry Americans. In the United States, organized crime flourished, funded by bootlegging. Al Capone from Chicago became famous. He was involved in the murder of at least thirty people and should be remembered as a mass murderer, yet his story often reads like that of a Robin Hood character.

Section 85 of the Indian Act[58] allows First Nations to ban alcohol on reserves. Several of our communities are now "dry." But the act of banning alcohol on-reserve doesn't seem to be having much success. The death rate continues. It seems that those communities that have banned alcohol are the ones that suffer the most. Bootleggers bring in alcohol by the truckload and it's our own people doing it. The bootleggers are frequently people who are better off than the rest of the community. They're frequently teachers, or other professionals, making a little extra by selling alcohol. Those who are extremely poor cannot afford a truck to drive to a community that has a liquor store and purchase $2,000 worth of liquor at once. So the poorer people, once again, are the hardest hit.

And so, because of bootleggers, banning alcohol by itself doesn't work. What happens is that the chief and council recognize that something needs to be done. They look at their options. The Indian Act allows them to ban alcohol. The Indian Act determines what the band bylaw can do. The First Nation can pass only bylaws that are allowed by the Indian Act, and the form of the bylaw is set out in the Act. Section 85.1 states that "the council of a band may make bylaws

(a) prohibiting the sale, barter, supply or man-ufacture of intoxicants on the reserve of the band;
(b) prohibiting any person from being intoxi-cated on the reserve;
(c) prohibiting any person from having intoxi-cants in his possession on the reserve; . . ."

Subsection 2 says that the band must first hold a special meeting and that a majority of electors at that meeting must vote in favour of the bylaw.

Subsection 4 sets out the punishment allowed. For the bootlegging part in s.85.1(a) above, the punishment allowed is a fine of up to $1,000 or imprisonment for a term not exceeding six months, or both. For a person being intoxicated on the reserve or having intoxicants, the Act allows for a fine of $100 or imprisonment for a term not exceeding three months, or both.

It looks like an easy fix. Chief and council hold a spe-cial meeting and the people agree that a solution to the alcohol problem is needed. Chief and council pass a band bylaw adopting the provisions of the Indian Act, and alcohol is banned.

Then they turn to the police to enforce the band bylaw.

What often happens next is that the police will get a call from someone in the community, saying that Joe is causing problems at house 27. The police go there and Joe is outside with his shirt off and he is extremely drunk and agitated. He's mad that they threw him out of the party. The person who phoned the police about Joe is often the person who gave Joe the alcohol in the first place, and when Joe got drunk on the alcohol they gave him and started to lose control, they phoned the police.

Joe is arrested and brought before the courts. The prosecutor and the defence lawyer have a discussion. If Joe has other charges along with the charge of being intoxicated on-reserve, the intox charge will frequently be withdrawn in exchange for a guilty plea to the Criminal Code charge. The intox charge becomes another item in the plea-bargain negotiations. No one takes it seriously.

It is extremely rare that a trial is ever run on a charge of intoxication. When a trial is run, the biggest hurdle for the Crown prosecutor is not to prove that the person was drunk or in breach of the bylaw, but that the bylaw was valid at the time. A certified copy of the bylaw must be filed with the court at trial, and the accused must be given at least seven days' notice that the Crown intends to file the certified copy. Certified copies of bylaws are not easy to obtain. Sometimes a prosecutor will file the document with the court and then ask the judge to give it back so that he can use it again in another trial.

Intoxicated-on-reserve charges are frequently handled by provincial Crown prosecutors, but they are properly the responsibility of federal prosecutors. Federal prosecutors most often prosecute drug charges; they don't want to travel to remote communities to prosecute bylaws, because the fine is usually only $100 and they seem to think it is not serious enough for them to take the time.

While imprisonment is possible for intoxicated-on-reserve convictions, it rarely ever happens. Judges don't want to send an Indigenous person to jail for something a white person living in the city could not be sent to jail for doing. To them, it is a matter of equality. That and, as I've mentioned earlier, the judges themselves are frequently drinkers who see nothing wrong with using alcohol.

And so we cannot depend upon the Indian Act and its very narrow limits on a First Nation's ability to control the most destructive force in our communities. We cannot depend upon the police to arrest every person who drinks or bootlegs. And we cannot depend upon the courts to enforce our bylaws.

We have now had decades of experience with band bylaws, police enforcement, and court-imposed fines, and the problem is only getting worse. Banning alcohol, thus far, just hasn't worked in our territory.

19. TREATMENT

The stories that we tell ourselves about alcohol are killing us. With a death rate of 50 per cent, something—anything—must be done to stop those stories. Because of the silence, because no one will talk about it, because we look the other way when we see our relatives begging in front of the liquor store or stumbling around in the community, that death rate continues.

If the chief and council were to take a firm stance and look at alcohol honestly and vigorously, they would recognize it as the most important issue of the day. Once it is looked at, it will be hard to look away from the graves and the despair. But first someone has to look and listen and someone has to speak.

Addictions counselling and treatment centres alone will not solve the problem of alcohol. We could definitely use more of them in our communities. In court, I frequently hear of people who are waiting months to get into a treatment centre. Anyone convicted twice of drinking and driving has to go to jail for thirty days. In Saskatchewan there is an option. They can go into the Impaired Driving Treatment Program (IDTP) instead of jail. Typically, the person pleads guilty and his lawyer asks the judge to order an IDTP report. The judge orders it. We adjourn the matter a month to get the report. We get the report and come back to court, and the report says there will be a space available seven or eight months later. It can easily take a full year, and often takes longer, from the time of the arrest until the person gets into a treatment program.

The situation can be worse for those who are severely addicted to alcohol. I know of a young man who, with the help of his Legal Aid lawyer, was admitted to the local detox centre. Detoxification is important for people who have been drinking steadily for a long time. Alcohol withdrawal is dangerous, and in severe cases people can have seizures that can lead to death. The young man was admitted. He stayed for the maximum ten days and then they told him he had to leave. He was trying to quit drinking and knew that if he went back to the place he normally stayed at, everyone there would be drinking. It was the weekend. He asked to stay until Monday, and against all regulations the staff bent the rules and let him stay. When he got out on Monday, he wanted to go straight to a treatment centre, but the only available centre was four hours away, in a city. Calls were made to the treatment centre but they couldn't take him, they wouldn't have room for another three months.

I don't know what happened to him. He wanted help when he was motivated to quit, and the help wasn't there when he needed it. I suspect that he went back out into the community and started drinking again, and it might be a long time until he is again motivated to quit.

I've also heard stories of probation officers who intervened in the process and drove clients to the city to have them admitted for treatment, knowing that when a person is motivated to change, things have to happen fast or the person will fall back down again.

It's all about the story we tell ourselves. I know a young man whose father died while in police custody. He was quite young when it happened and has grown up telling himself that it is his purpose in life to make sure those policemen—who, he tells himself, killed his father—are brought to justice. He imagines, over and over again, what he would do to the officers if he ever found them, how he would do to them what they did to his father.

He's a good worker. He has a good job and a family, and he loves his family and wants to look after them. But, as he puts it, he has a monkey on his back. He can't seem to get away from drinking. Whenever things get too stressful in his life, he finds a bottle. He has struggled for many years to put alcohol away, knowing what it does to families. But he keeps telling himself the story of vengeance and justice and keeps a little fire of anger burning. As long as he keeps telling himself that story, the anger is going to stay. Anger doesn't make us strong. It makes us weak, especially if we carry it for a long time. As long as my friend keeps telling himself that story that he carries, he is not going to develop the strength he needs to overcome alcohol. He needs a different story.

20. LEADERSHIP

recently read two interesting studies. In the first study, carried out on the west coast of British Columbia, researchers were trying to find out why some Aboriginal communities had higher rates of suicide than other communities. When they looked closely, they learned that in those communities with lower rates of suicide, the leadership was actively trying to make things better. They had launched land claims and were politically involved. In the communities with the highest levels of suicide, there were no land claims, no one was negotiating with government, no one was trying to make things better. People in these communities lived in two separate stories. In one story there was hope. In the other there was no reason to continue to live.[59]

The other interesting study came out of the United States. Researchers connected the murder rate with satisfaction with the president. In periods when there was a high satisfaction with the president, when his approval ratings were highest, the murder rate was at its lowest, and when people were the least satisfied with the president, the murder rate was at its highest.[60]

What leadership does is very important. The people are watching. If leadership behaves responsibly, is not involved in scandal, works diligently for the betterment of the people, and creates a story of dignity and morals, then the people will see that and participate in the story. If leadership is drunk, involved in corruption, out to better only itself, the people are watching, and the story that is created will be the story that the people live.

To solve alcohol we need sober leaders.

Our traditional teachings tell us not to preach. We are not to go around telling other people how to live, because we don't know anything. We each develop our own understanding and no one's understanding is greater or lesser than anyone else's. In the past in our traditional way, we learned things by watching others. We were encouraged to watch and not ask questions: how to skin an animal, how to make a fire, how to tan a hide, how to make snowshoes, how to make a paddle. We sat and watched and that was how we learned. How to clean and fillet a fish—we watched how our mother did it, we watched our grandma, our auntie or our uncle, and we took a little from each of them until we developed our own way to clean a fish. We were encouraged to watch, to pay attention, and to learn. There were no strict regulations, no set method, no instructions written down somewhere, no single way of doing.

We also learned how to pay attention. If we came from a family with grandparents and parents who carried themselves with dignity, who behaved morally and ethically, we learned to be good people. If we lived in a good story, if all around us everyone behaved in a good way, we developed our own personal story to match the stories of everyone around us.

20. LEADERSHIP

When it comes to alcohol, we learned to drink by watching everyone around us. If the drinking story we come from is one of drinking to extreme, then that is how our story begins. Our story, our personal story, the one we tell ourselves, is connected to the story of our family, our community, and our leadership. We grow our personal story, based on all the stories of all the people to whom we are connected.

In our traditional way of knowing, we understood that everything is connected to everything else. The phrase "All My Relations" that we say at the end of our prayers isn't just talking about our aunts and uncles and cousins, it also refers to all the plants and animals, the water, the sky, the four directions, and everything else to which we are related.

Our traditional teachings tell us that trees are related to the earth and to the sky, that every living thing has water in it, and that the people are more important than the person. It's all about the relationship, about connection.

When a person is in a position of leadership, everyone is watching all the time. If the chief and council pass a bylaw prohibiting alcohol and then go out drinking, leave the community and go to the casino or a nightclub in the city, the people will see that, and we can pass all the bylaws we want, bring in all the police we want to enforce the bylaw, fine people, and even send people to jail, and the people will not obey the bylaw.

We do not make change in the world by preaching and passing laws. We change the world with what we do. If any of us stays sober, walks in the world in a good way, the people will see us walking and say to themselves,

"Look at her, see her walking, she doesn't have a hang-over. I want to be like that." And she saves a life.

If we drink, people will see us and say to themselves, "Look at him, he can drink, so can I." And we take a life.

21. THE STORYTELLER

magine our traditional way of being here on Turtle Island. We lived as a community of hunters and gatherers constantly on the move. To decide in which direction we wanted to go, we sent scouts who went out and looked over the land, then came back and reported to the people. Maybe they said, "To the west there are plenty of ripe berries, to the north there is a herd of buffalo, to the east the wild turnips are ready, and to the south there has been a huge fire and there is nothing there this year." Then the chief spoke to the people, consulted with the thinkers, the headmen or lead women, and made a decision: they would first go west and harvest the berries—by then the buffalo would be a little fatter—and after they finished with the buffalo, they would harvest the turnips.

Today's society is much the same. We are constantly moving—we are advancing, becoming. Yet, many of our leaders don't seem to be leading. It seems that the politician looks at the polls and figures out in which direction the people are headed, and then runs out front and pretends to be leading.

The thinkers have stopped talking to the people. The thinkers in this society are the scientists and the academics. They tend to talk only to themselves, and have even created complex language that only they understand. The jargon created by each separate field of study has become so extreme that even a scientist or academic from a related field often cannot understand what is being said.

The scouts today are the artists. We go out in our imagination and imagine the future and bring it back for the people in our books and our songs and our art. For example, George Orwell's novel *Nineteen Eighty-Four* was published in 1949. In it, he predicted Big Brother and constant government surveillance. His predictions have come to pass in many ways. Look at the Edward Snowden affair and the recent Harper government's attempt to spy on its citizens, or the closed-circuit TV networks set up in major cities like London and Chicago, which keep a close eye on us, watching. Big Brothers of all sorts are definitely out there. But yet, we do not live in the world that the character O'Brien describes as the "picture of the future" in *Nineteen Eighty-Four*:

> There will be no curiosity, no enjoyment of the process of life. All competing pleasures will be destroyed. But always—do not forget this, Winston—always there will be the intoxication of power, constantly increasing and constantly growing subtler. Always, at every moment, there will be the thrill of victory, the sensation of trampling on an enemy who is helpless. If you want a picture of the future, imagine a boot stamping on a human face—for ever.[61]

21. THE STORYTELLER

The reason we do not live in the world Orwell predicted is because he predicted it. Every time the government infringes upon our privacy, we reference Big Brother and demand that the government stop because we know, thanks to Orwell and our artists, where that type of surveillance will lead.

Today, we seem to be short of good scouts. Many of the artists don't seem to realize their role: to protect us, to go out as a scout to warn us what is coming. If the artists imagine only violence and sex, we cannot complain if we live in a very violent and pornographic society. If, in all our stories, in our movies and television shows, we always imagine alcohol as a central part of our social structure, we cannot complain if everyone around us is drunk. This is what we have imagined for the people. These are the stories we've given them to live by.

However, we can be thankful that there are some artists out there who are scouts, who give us stories of goodness to live by, scouts who live without alcohol, who show us a path to follow. Buffy St. Marie speaks about how she doesn't use drugs or alcohol; Richard Wagamese is proud of his sobriety and sanity. In *The Reason You Walk,* Wab Kinew writes of how both he and his father left self-destructive behaviours behind, choosing instead to live without alcohol. Tracey Lindberg, author of *Birdie*, and Richard Van Camp, author of *The Lesser Blessed,* share their words of abstinence with us in letters near the end of this story.

There are starting to be more and more artists. If these and other artists go out, scout for us, and imagine a future without intoxication, give us art and stories that are more than about sex, drugs, and violence, stories where ethics and morals and values are more important than immediate gratification and making money, perhaps the rest of our people can and will begin to move in that direction.

22. HEALING

As I see it, our task as we go forward is not the healing of those individuals in our society who are most hurt by alcohol. We keep trying to do that. We sentence them to jail to make them pay attention to the fact that their alcohol-induced violence is not acceptable. We put them on probation or conditional sentences with conditions to remain sober. We put them on court orders to attend for counselling and addictions treatment. But then they come back from the prisons and rehab centres into communities and homes where excessive alcohol use is normal. Working at healing only the individual, then, will never be successful.

When I was at the post office the other day, a man approached me. He obviously had been drinking, but was far from falling-down drunk. He was still making sense. He wanted to know if I could help him go to jail. I've known him for many years. For most of his life he was a hard-core drunk. I have prosecuted him several times for things he did while he was intoxicated. This is a man with a long criminal record, including a manslaughter conviction when he was quite young. In the past I have recommended to the sentencing judge that this man be sent to jail because it would be pointless to put him on conditions in the community.

I've seen him around on the streets, and he frequently comes and talks to me. For the last several months he has been working very hard on trying to stay sober. I remember seeing him a while ago and he wanted to let me know that he had been sober for about a month, that he had been to detox and that he expected to go into treatment soon. I told him that I was proud of him.

That day at the post office, the reason he wanted to go to jail was because he knew he was going to die if he stayed on the streets. He was very disappointed in himself. He had been to a treatment centre for over a month and had just got back to the community. He felt so good about himself that when he got back with his friends, he started drinking with them.

The only option that he could see to stay sober was if I could arrange it so that he could go to jail. In jail he would be away from his friends, away from alcohol, in a safe, secure place. He was aware that if he stayed on the life path he was on, he was going to die. But his life path wasn't his alone. It was entangled with everyone around him. His life path was the streets, the liquor store and the bars, and his community of friends. It was drinking houses and park benches and bottles of wine. The problem is not just him. It's much larger than the individual. But this man wasn't feeling sorry for himself. He wasn't blaming anyone other than himself. He was looking for a solution to his situation. He was trying to save his own life, and the only option that he could see was that maybe I could help him go to jail.

22. HEALING

To show that this isn't just the problem of healing individuals, but that it's much greater than the individual, let me give you another story, this one at the other end of the drinking spectrum. Another young man I know grew up away from alcohol. His life was the trapline. But while he was out there, he experienced a trauma: his close friend fell through the ice and drowned, and he was not able to save him, despite his best efforts. Alcohol was not involved. It was just one of those things that happen sometimes. After that, he didn't want to go back to the trapline. So he stayed in town.

But in town there was not much for a young man to do. Everyone around him drank. At first he stayed sober, didn't like alcohol, didn't want to be like everyone else. At the age of eighteen, he had never touched alcohol. When everyone was drinking, he stayed away, stayed by himself. He was the only person he knew who was sober. Eventually he decided to join everyone else. Being sober meant that he had to be alone. It was loneliness that drew him into partying; he began drinking so he could be a part of the community.

I've known him for over a decade. He's a good worker, always has a job, takes care of himself and others. But today he is messaging me: he's looking for advice on what to do about the criminal charges he now faces.

Our traditional understanding tells us that everything is connected to everything else, that we are all related, and what happens to one of us affects us all. We cannot heal the individual without healing the community. So, how do we do that? How do we heal our communities? We can't court order a community to abstain.

This is what I think we must do and we must do it now. *We have to change the story that we tell ourselves about ourselves and about alcohol.*

Even though we are faced with the tradition of "Don't preach. Be an example. Don't tell people how to live; show them how to live," we are, at the same time, living in a modern world where we are told everyday how to live our lives through media, through advertising, through movies. Alcohol is everywhere: it is advertised constantly and not just in the paid advertisements. I frequently hear "news" stories on public radio about wine making, whiskey tasting, and beer brewing. Usually the reporter is interviewing someone who "crafts" alcohol, be it wine or beer, and the story is about how this new local product is different from all the other products. Or the story is about the new whiskey and how taste is changing away from Scottish brands towards Canadian, how the Japanese have discovered whiskey, and how worldwide sales are increasing. This is how engrained alcohol is in the *kiciwamanawak* story and now in ours—how "normal" it appears. Imagine if the reporter was talking to drug dealers or those who were "crafting" a new version of cocaine. We guard against these stories, for we know the harm they do to us. So what about these stories of alcohol that are now seen in our everyday world?

Indeed, social media have now picked up and normalized the alcohol story. We frequently see our friends post-Thirsty Thursday, or Wine O'clock, or pictures of them and their friends with bottles or glasses raised toward the camera.

We cannot stop the alcohol story that *kiciwamanawak* tell from spreading. We can't ask our public broadcasters to stop doing stories about wine tastings. Everyone has the right to speak, and so do we. Censorship will not do.

But changing the story doesn't mean stopping, or censoring, the story that's out there; it means telling a new story, a better story. How about we spread the story that we are proud of our traditional culture and that it is a culture of sobriety? I would love to see a Facebook posting that said, "I am proud to be Cree, proud to be sober." Or, "Sobriety proves you love your family." Imagine all the possibilities to tell a new and better story about who we are.

Perhaps we will get to the point where we will see truth-telling about alcohol, and perhaps this too is a way to change the story about alcohol. The next time one of our relatives gets run over by a drunk driver, or stabbed to death in a drunken brawl, instead of offering condolences, we will speak instead of how our cousin was murdered by alcohol. This will be the new Facebook status update until the story changes.

23. COMMUNITY

Despite the seriousness of the alcohol problem, despite the fact that we have a death rate from alcohol of one in two people, despite all the problems I have outlined thus far, it needs to be stated that not all of us are drunk in our communities.

There is another statistic, but this one is rarely mentioned. It is this: *there are more people in the Aboriginal population who are completely abstinent than in the general population.* Studies have shown that there are twice as many Aboriginal people who do not drink at all, compared with the rest of Canada.[62] A recent study found that 35 per cent of Aboriginal people do not drink at all.[63] It seems we either drink hard or not at all. Many of the completely sober are people who have returned to Native spirituality, to what has been referred to as the "Red Road."

Several of the people who are abstinent follow the Christian tradition. And then, there is a huge body of people who are neither Christian nor traditionalist who, for their own reasons, have decided not to drink. I know a man in a far northern community who told me he had been a drinker. He drank a couple of times when he was fifteen or sixteen and didn't like it. He was sixty-five when he told me. He also said that to his knowledge, his wife had never had a drink of alcohol.

I know of another family from a community on the west side of the province who moved a few kilometres away from their community and lived off the land to get away from the drinking. They had cows and chickens, and they hunted and fished and stayed sober. But all their children were drawn back to the community and the partying. I came across this family because one of their sons was in extreme trouble with the law.

The court party flies into remote communities across the North. In a community of 1,800, we frequently see about 400 people who come to court over and over again, either as accused persons or as victims. The other 1,400 we never see. It's easy to fall into believing that the entire community is messed up if all we see are those who come to court.

But there are communities within communities. The people who come to court over and over again usually belong to a subcommunity of heavy drinkers. They all know each other, drink together, hang out together, and party together. They know who the bootleggers are, know when the booze is coming, know where the party is going to be tonight. All their friends belong to the sub-community, and often all their families belong as well. Within these subcommunities, drinking has become the central part of their existence.

Within these subcommunities, the death rate is extreme. I ran a murder trial a few years back. At the preliminary hearing I had fifteen civilian witnesses. They all knew each other, all associated with each other. After the preliminary hearing, the accused was committed to stand trial. Between the time of the preliminary hearing and the trial, three of the witnesses had died. One was killed in a car accident in which alcohol was involved, and two died from alcohol poisoning.

The majority of us are not heavy drinkers and so are not involved with the courts. Most of us who are sober are silently sober. We do not speak of our sobriety. Most of us are caught in the tradition of not telling anyone what to do. It's a powerful tradition that is fundamental to our culture. But just because we cannot tell anyone to sober up doesn't mean we must remain silent. We don't have to go quietly to the graveyard. We can speak. We can speak of our own sobriety. We can speak of our people's history of sobriety. We can tell sober stories.

niwâhkomakanak, we have been waiting since 1875, when we sent the letter to the Treaty commissioner for *kiciwamanawak* to do something about alcohol. We can quit waiting. They are not going to do anything. We are stuck with the problem. It is up to us to fix things. We are the ones who go over and over to the graveyard and bury our relatives. We visit our relatives in the hospital. We experience the black eyes, the broken teeth, the stab wounds, and the brain injuries. I am surprised by the number of people I meet in the court system who have an acquired brain injury as a result of getting hit in the head with a baseball bat or a board or a rock during a drunken brawl.

I recently met a man named Ron Capps. He was in five wars in ten years and of course experienced PTSD. He decided to survive. He now runs a program for veterans who use storytelling to help them with their disabilities. In the Veterans Writing Project, veterans learn to write their stories as part of their treatment. They can shred the story or share it, but the healing comes from the writing. This project speaks to the power of story and its ability to heal.

Ron Capps said something that really stuck in my mind. He said that "wars will be fought as long as the people find them exciting and they won't quit until they are tired of it."[64]

We must ask ourselves, *niwâhkomakanak*, Do we continue drinking because we find it exciting, or have we had enough? Are we tired enough of going to the graveyard, are we tired enough of the violence and abuse, are we tired of the hangovers?

If the answer is yes, if we are tired of dying, then we can begin to work at changing the story.

Changing the story means that the sober people in our communities tell their story of sobriety. And you begin to tell your story.

24. THE SOBER HOUSE AND THE SOBER COMMUNITY

An idea has emerged from my talks with our people. We know that the hardest part about quitting drinking is losing all your friends or finding out who your real friends are. We frequently go to treatment centres for rehab and then return to the same community, to the same family, to the same house where all our drinking occurred. It usually takes about four months before those friends, those relatives, stop bugging us to come drinking with them: "Come on, Bro, a drink or two won't hurt you none." One of the reasons for the dismal success rate of treatment is that we often give in to pressure, whether that pressure is direct, someone asking us to come drink with them, or the pressure comes just from the fact that everyone around us is drinking all the time and we feel left out.

The idea is for a Sober House sign. It borrows from the Block Parent campaign. If you have a sober house, if you are one of the 35 per cent of our people who never use alcohol, you put a Sober House sign on your door and people will know that you welcome sober people to come and join you. For a person in your community who suddenly finds herself alone, friendless, and maybe even cut out of her own family, your sober house might be her only refuge.

A safe place, a cup of tea, someone to talk to, someone who understands: the experience of what a healthy life and a healthy home look like would be, for many of our relatives, something superior to any treatment centre.

My dream is that instead of sending our people away for treatment, we turn our communities into treatment centres. I don't imagine going back to a time before alcohol came here. Instead, I imagine a future for our children and grandchildren, a healthy place where we are not experiencing the cycles of trauma and grief and drinking to overcome the grief, leading to more trauma. We get to that imagined future by changing the story that we tell ourselves and each other—our sons, daughters, sisters, brothers, cousins, aunties, uncles—today. Writers Tracey Lindberg and Richard Van Camp have offered to help get us started. These are their stories, their letters that they chose to share with us.

PART 3

LETTERS FROM OUR
SCOUTS, THE ARTISTS

A LETTER FROM
TRACEY LINDBERG

Dear Harold and the People of Treaty 6,
   I stopped drinking about 25 years ago. Until then, I engaged in what was quite likely binge drinking. My relationship with booze began in grade 8. Boys with licenses picked up girls without and gave us alcohol. My first drink was vodka. Then rye. Then peach schnapps. Then beer. My first vomit was, too.

My family home did not feel like a safe space, to me. I was sexually assaulted repeatedly by a friend of the family for much of what would have been a childhood. My response was addiction: I ate. And ate. Until I reformed and deformed my body. It was safer than being hunted.

My sexual assault ended when we moved to a new town. It was and is a beautiful northern town. With that beauty came a culture of hockey, booze, and binging. From the age of 14 onward, I could find a party every night, if I wanted to. Most certainly, we found or made parties on the weekend. Indoors, outdoors, halls, rinks, houses, farmyards, barns, quonsets: drinking lived in your home, but was also a place you could visit as much as you wanted.

Alcohol, for an introvert, allowed me to say things that were not allowed, do things that were unconventional, and the luxury of sloppy, friendly touch among drunk comrades. All celebrations and upsets were treatable with booze. Exams over? Drink! Won't see your Uni friends until fall? Party. Got dumped? Chug. By the time I went to graduate school, I was drinking/binging two days a week. By the time I was practising law, three days a week. At least.

Drinking made the little free time that I had expand and made all of the deprivation (time with family, gatherings, meaningful conversations, births of/deaths of family members) tolerable. In the practice of law, and as the only Indigenous person in the firm that I worked for, alcohol became the lubricant through which I could unpeel my layer of Other and become One with the Firm. It was me, and I made a choice, and the choice was to make friends through boozing with them.

In my first year of practising law, I started working with a Nation which governed through hereditary leadership. One of my mentors, a Cree lawyer, said to me something to the effect of "How can you know how to protect something that you don't know? You need to attend the ceremonies/live on the land in order to know what you are fighting for." It is, to this day, the truth that allowed me the possibility of health. Of whole.

I started going to ceremonies. Once in a while, someone would come into the ceremony who had been recently drinking. The rest of us in the ceremony would physically and emotionally have to provide that which the attendee could not provide: strength, prayers, cleanliness. Quite literally, I felt like I was paying when the person who had been drinking came into the ceremony. I never said anything, just attended and prayed, because that is what we do.

One day, it hit me: people were having to pay for whatever I brought into the lodge, too. That was the near end. I made a decision because I loved to drink. I made a decision because I needed to drink. This, I knew, was going to get harder and harder to do as time went by. This, I also knew, was a choice at that time (a luxury, the choice to stop) but that in the future, it might not be something I could stop.

So I stopped. I continued going to ceremonies. I felt good. I quit drinking entirely. I felt better.

And I had to learn how to socialize (I am still not good at it) without alcohol, had to learn to hug without alcohol, and had to define and parse my spare time without alcohol. I do miss the denizens of the bars I haunted. Do miss that easy drunky friendship amongst drunken strangers. Miss the excitement of live music in small rooms, yelled conversations, and weird semi-hallucinatory observations.

What I know now: today, not one of those denizens is a friend. You will make your introversion worse if you don't take care of it sober. People (communities, Nations, peers, and strangers) know that competency is quite often in the passenger seat next to sobriety.

The Nation that I work with never *required* that I quit. I quit because they don't drink. Because I wanted no one to have to pay my way in ceremony but me. Because I wanted to be a sober advocate for them. Because I wanted to be free.

Freedom is walking away and doing better. I'm free.

Tracey Lindberg
March 2016

A LETTER FROM RICHARD VAN CAMP

My son,

You are almost two as I write this. Mahsi cho for choosing your mother and me. She's an incredible mom, hey? She's my lighthouse and you two are my everything. I was born to marry her and we were born to carry you, hold you, and raise you to the best of our abilities. I pray you are a peacemaker. The world needs more of them.

I've been asked to write about why I don't drink. My answer is simple: I'm terrified of its power over our people and, as I write this, alcohol is literally drinking our family to death. It's eaten us alive for decades and will continue to do so. Maybe one day I'll tell you about our family reunion which broke my heart. Or maybe I'll tell about when I was a guard for the RCMP and I saw so many families being ruined by alcohol and its patient and cunning ways.

They say some families shouldn't drink, and ours is one of them. I pray that you respect alcohol the same way I do: with fear.

It is stronger than love. I have seen it. While it has you, it has you.

In this year of 2016 so many of us from the Northern communities have decided to focus on culture, language, healing because we've been through so much. We want better for our families and for our future and for the world.

I never want to scare you with my words or actions. I want to be accountable to your mother and to you. I never want you to see the wolf that is in our family: hiding, waiting, ugly.

May our house always be safe; may our home always be a place of stories, music, reading, sharing, and helping.

It took so much suffering to reach here.

I love you and even the word "love"—well, it doesn't do justice to what I feel for you. I ache to hold you, to sniff you, to kiss, to nuzzle and carry you. My hands ache for you.

This is our love and our life and I am proud to be a son, a father, a husband, a brother, and a friend that anyone can depend on.

And it's time to look forward to the best that life has to offer: travel, friends, family, work that inspires, adventure.

Alcohol is the dream killer of all people. I promise you.

As I write this it's bath time. Your mother and you are laughing, singing. The geese are already returning to Edmonton. One honked over our house this afternoon.

All is as it should be for our family.
May it always be this way.

I love you, Edzazii.
Your father,
Richard Van Camp
March 2016

PART 4

NIYÂK: FOR THE FUTURE

WÎSAHKICÂHK RETURNS TO FIND OUT HE IS STORY

Kayâs, Wîsahkicâhk had been around for a long time. He went away when things started to get rough for our people because he didn't want to be blamed for the things he saw coming. He was gone for quite a while. Some people said he was hiding in the mountains in Alberta. Some said he went to the happy hunting grounds to hang out with the ancestors.

Anyway, he decided to come back, just to check it out, see how the people were doing. The first person he met was a young boy, maybe thirteen, fourteen years old, walking down the street with a cell phone in his hand, not paying attention to where he was going. He bumped into Wîsahkicâhk.

Wîsahkicâhk said, "Excuse me!"

The boy looked up at the strange man he'd bumped into. He said, "Who are you?"

"I'm Wîsahkicâhk," Wîsahkicâhk said with a big, proud smile.

"You're not real," said the boy, looking back down at his phone to see if someone liked his post on Facebook.

"Of course I'm real," said Wîsahkicâhk. "I'm right here. Right in front of you."

"If you're Wîsahkicâhk, then you're not real. You're just a story." The boy started texting and walked away, still not paying any attention to where he was going—lost in the cyberworld.

"I'm not just a story," Wîsahkicâhk said to himself. "I'm real." He pinched his cheek to make sure. Yep, he was real. He could feel the pinch.

Next, he met a woman hurrying along with a baby in a stroller. Again he introduced himself all proud-like. "Good morning," he said, "my name is Wîsahkicâhk."

The woman stopped for a second. She didn't have time for this nonsense. She had things to do. "Then you should go to the school, to the Native Studies department. They have a course there on traditional stories, it's all about you." And she walked away.

"I'm not a story," Wîsahkicâhk yelled after her, but she just kept walking, in a hurry, going somewhere important, like to the shopping mall.

"I'm not a story," he repeated this time to himself. "I'm not."

But everyone he met that day said the same thing. "You're not real. You're just a story." And he couldn't convince any one of them any differently.

He came to a park. There were trees there and grass. It seemed like a good place to be. He sat down on the grass and began to think about what the people had said. What if I am just a story? he thought. What if I just made myself up?

He tried to figure it out. He'd been around for a long, long time, but he hadn't been here forever. He had a beginning. He knew his mom, Cihcipistikwân. He remembered being a boy, he remembered his little brother mahikan from back then. But that didn't prove anything. Stories have beginnings.

He remembered all the things he had done, all the tricks he had played on the animals. But that didn't make him real. That was just humour, and stories can be funny. In fact, the best stories are funny.

"But I had an impact on the world. That should make me real," he muttered to himself. "The things I did make me real. It was me who used the mud Muskrat brought up at the time of the flood to make Turtle Island. That's a pretty important thing to have done. Yep, I'm real, alright." He patted the ground beside him. "This wouldn't be here if not for me."

But he wasn't convinced.

Just because he pinched himself and felt something didn't make him real. Maybe in the story, he was supposed to feel things. Same thing with the ground: maybe in the story, he was supposed to feel the ground. Maybe it was all story, including himself. Maybe the people were just story too.

He really started to think.

He sat there for days, wrapped in a blanket, and didn't look up. Sometimes people went by. Mostly they looked the other way and walked faster. But sometimes they threw some money at him, loonies and toonies and quarters.

It might just be that he was only story. He went through his whole life, every little thing. He squirmed a little bit when he remembered burning his ass on a hot rock, and he sat up a little straighter when he remembered how Weasel saved him from the wetiko that time when the monster had him tied up and was taking a nap before he ate him. How all the other animals were afraid of the wetiko, but Weasel was brave and ran down the sleeping monster's throat and bit off the string that held its heart, and Wîsahkicâhk had rewarded Weasel's bravery by painting him pure white, except for the tip of his tail that he had held him by while he painted him.

Good times.

And Fox, and all the fun they had had together. Good times, for sure.

But what did it all mean in the end?

If it was all just story, if he was just story, what good was it?

And the end, how was the story going to end?

He'd been around for a long time, but he wasn't going to be here forever. He was already starting to feel old. His hair was still long but it was turning white, and his teeth were feeling a little loose, and he couldn't see as far as he used to, and sometimes when someone said something he would have to say "Huh," because he didn't hear them the first time.

He started thinking really hard then, urgently. He thought back all the way to the beginning when his mom had that thing going on with the snakes and his dad had chopped off her head and she had chased him and his little brother mahikan, her head rolling after them.

He thought back even before that to when he was born. Someone had stuck a nipple in his mouth and when he sucked, warm milk squirted into his mouth.

At the same time he heard sounds and he had put those two together, the taste of warm milk in his mouth and the sounds his mother made, and he had begun to learn language. Slowly his understanding had grown. With each new experience he added to the body of understanding. He made sense out of the world with his mind. Bit by bit, every time he experienced something new, he checked it against what he already knew and if it fit together he kept it.

But . . .

Wîsahkicâhk looked up.

He looked at the sky.

He almost cried when he realized that if anywhere along the way, if he made a mistake, everything he learned after would be wrong, all the way back to that first taste of milk in his mouth and the sounds his mother made. He couldn't prove that anything was true. If his body of understanding was wrong, if the things he thought he knew were not correct, and he relied on his body of understanding to learn new things, then the new thing would be wrong too.

He almost gave up.

But . . .

There was something still not resolved. There was something else going on. He thought back again to when that warm milk was squirted in his mouth, before he knew language, or before he thought he understood language; there was something there—something without words.

There was a message there, and it wasn't until he learned words that he was able to describe the message. And the message said, "You are destined for greatness."

That's what the message said on good days. Some days all the message said was "Hold on."

The message had been inside of him before he came to this world. If it was there before . . .

Maybe there was an after.

If there was an after . . . But he couldn't be certain there was an after, only a before.

But he couldn't prove either. It was good enough that he had a purpose. He was destined for greatness.

But . . .

He was getting old. He was going to keep getting old and someday he was going to get sick and die and he would be buried and the worms would eat him. And after the worms ate him it didn't matter what he had done in his life.

All of a sudden the message felt like a cruel joke.

Any greatness he could achieve would only feed the worms.

He thought about the people, all the people he had met since the beginning of people. They all seemed to have the same message. They all seemed to carry it whether they said it or not. You could tell just by looking at them, how they stood up straight, how they refused to quit. He remembered all those things the people had gone through, the Trail of Tears, Wounded Knee, the cold and the hunger and the scorn, and how through it all the people had stayed strong. They knew somewhere inside each of them that they were supposed to be great.

So all of humanity has the message.

Why?

Was it a cruel joke on all of us?

152

We are all going to be worm food and it won't matter what any one of us did in our lives, won't matter how much money we made, or how famous we became, or if we invented atomic bombs or went to the moon: we were going to be worm food, and the worms would eat our greatness along with our bodies.

So why does all of humanity have that message? Why does it drive people to achieve fame, or make a lot of money, or invent things, or go to the moon?

All of a sudden Wîsahkicâhk jumped up.

He started running around, yelling at the top of his lungs.

"It's not me."

"It's not me."

"I'm not the one," he yelled.

He ran up to a young girl walking by. He scared her and she backed away, looking around to see if anyone was watching.

"It's not me," he said. "And it's not you." He wasn't yelling anymore so the girl stood still and listened.

"We are not destined for greatness by ourselves." He told her, his voice excited. "All of humanity has the message, so it's humanity that's destined for greatness."

He started yelling again, and the last time anyone saw him, he was running down the street, screaming: "Humanity is destined for greatness. Humanity is destined for greatness."

Humanity is destined for greatness, that is why we travelled across the universe as little dots of blue light to come here and experience this wonderful story.

APPENDIX: TREATY NO. 6

TREATY 6 BETWEEN HER MAJESTY THE QUEEN

AND THE PLAIN AND WOOD CREE INDIANS

AND

OTHER TRIBES OF INDIANS

ARTICLES OF A TREATY made and concluded near Carlton on the 23rd day of August and on the 28th day of said month, respectively, and near Fort Pitt on the 9th day of September, in the year of Our Lord one thousand eight hundred and seventy-six, between Her Most Gracious Majesty the Queen of Great Britain and Ireland, by Her Commissioners, the Honourable Alexander Morris, Lieutenant-Governor of the Province of Manitoba and the Northwest Territories, and the Honourable James McKay, and the Honourable William Joseph Christie, of the one part, and the Plain and Wood Cree and the other Tribes of Indians, inhabitants of the country within the limits hereinafter defined and described by their Chiefs, chosen and named as hereinafter mentioned, of the other part.

Whereas the Indians inhabiting the said country have, pursuant to an appointment made by the said Commissioners, been convened at meetings at Fort Carlton, Fort Pitt and Battle River, to deliberate upon certain matters of interest to Her Most Gracious Majesty, of the one part, and the said Indians of the other.

And whereas the said Indians have been notified and informed by Her Majesty's said Commissioners that it is the desire of Her Majesty to open up for settlement, immigration and such other purposes as to Her Majesty may seem meet, a tract of country bounded and described as hereinafter mentioned, and to obtain the consent thereto of Her Indian subjects inhabiting the said tract, and to make a treaty and arrange with them, so that there may be peace and good will between them and Her Majesty, and that they may know and be assured of what allowance they are to count upon and receive from Her Majesty's bounty and benevolence.

And whereas the Indians of the said tract, duly convened in council, as aforesaid, and being requested by Her Majesty's said Commissioners to name certain Chiefs and Headmen, who should be authorized on their behalf to conduct such negotiations and sign any treaty to be founded thereon, and to become responsible to Her Majesty for their faithful performance by their respective Bands of such obligations as shall be assumed by them, the said Indians have thereupon named for that purpose, that is to say, representing the Indians who make the treaty at Carlton, the several Chiefs and Councillors who have subscribed hereto, and representing the Indians who make the treaty at Fort Pitt, the several Chiefs and Councillors who have subscribed hereto.

And thereupon, in open council, the different Bands having presented their Chiefs to the said Commissioners as the Chiefs and Headmen, for the purposes aforesaid, of the respective Bands of Indians inhabiting the said district hereinafter described.

And whereas, the said Commissioners then and there received and acknowledged the persons so presented as Chiefs and Headmen, for the purposes aforesaid, of the respective Bands of Indians inhabiting the said district hereinafter described.

And whereas, the said Commissioners have proceeded to negotiate a treaty with the said Indians, and the same has been finally agreed upon and concluded, as follows, that is to say:

The Plain and Wood Cree Tribes of Indians, and all other the Indians inhabiting the district hereinafter described and defined, do hereby cede, release, surrender and yield up to the Government of the Dominion of Canada, for Her Majesty the Queen and Her successors forever, all their rights, titles and privileges, whatsoever, to the lands included within the following limits, that is to say:

Commencing at the mouth of the river emptying into the northwest angle of Cumberland Lake; thence westerly up the said river to its source; thence on a straight line in a westerly direction to the head of Green Lake; thence northerly to the elbow in the Beaver River; thence down the said river northerly to a point twenty miles from the said elbow; thence in a westerly direction, keeping on a line generally parallel with the said Beaver River (above the elbow), and about twenty miles distant therefrom, to the source of the said river; thence northerly to the north-easterly point of the south shore of Red Deer Lake, continuing westerly along the said shore to the western limit thereof; and thence due west to the Athabasca River; thence up the said river, against the stream, to the Jaspar House, in the Rocky Mountains; thence on a course south-easterly, following the easterly range of the mountains, to the source of the main branch of the Red Deer River; thence down the said river, with the stream, to the junction therewith of the outlet of the river, being the outlet of the Buffalo Lake; thence due east twenty miles; thence on a straight line south-eastwardly to the mouth of the said Red Deer River on the south branch of the Saskatchewan River; thence eastwardly and northwardly, following on the boundaries of the tracts conceded by the several treaties numbered four and five to the place of beginning.

And also, all their rights, titles and privileges whatsoever to all other lands wherever situated in the North-west Territories, or in any other Province or portion of Her Majesty's Dominions, situated and being within the Dominion of Canada.

The tract comprised within the lines above described embracing an area of 121,000 square miles, be the same more or less.

To have and to hold the same to Her Majesty the Queen and Her successors forever.

And Her Majesty the Queen hereby agrees and undertakes to lay aside reserves for farming lands, due respect being had to lands at present cultivated by the said Indians, and other reserves for the benefit of the said Indians, to be administered and dealt with for them by Her Majesty's Government of the Dominion of Canada; provided, all such reserves shall not exceed in all one square mile for each family of five, or in that proportion for larger or smaller families, in manner following, that is to say: that the Chief Superintendent of Indian Affairs shall depute and send a suitable person to determine and set apart the reserves for each band, after consulting with the Indians thereof as to the locality which may be found to be most suitable for them.

Provided, however, that Her Majesty reserves the right to deal with any settlers within the bounds of any lands reserved for any Band as She shall deem fit, and also that the aforesaid reserves of land, or any interest therein, may be sold or otherwise disposed of by Her Majesty's Government for the use and benefit of the said Indians entitled thereto, with their consent first had and obtained; and with a view to show the satisfaction of Her Majesty with the behaviour and good conduct of Her Indians, She hereby, through Her Commissioners, makes them a present of twelve dollars for each man, woman and child belonging to the Bands here represented, in extinguishment of all claims heretofore preferred.

And further, Her Majesty agrees to maintain schools for instruction in such reserves hereby made as to Her Government of the Dominion of Canada may seem advisable, whenever the Indians of the reserve shall desire it.

Her Majesty further agrees with Her said Indians that within the boundary of Indian reserves, until otherwise determined by Her Government of the Dominion of Canada, no intoxicating liquor shall be allowed to be introduced or sold, and all laws now in force, or hereafter to be enacted, to preserve Her Indian subjects inhabiting the reserves or living elsewhere within Her Northwest Territories from the evil influence of the use of intoxicating liquors, shall be strictly enforced.

APPENDIX

Her Majesty further agrees with Her said Indians that they, the said Indians, shall have right to pursue their avocations of hunting and fishing throughout the tract surrendered as hereinbefore described, subject to such regulations as may from time to time be made by Her Government of Her Dominion of Canada, and saving and excepting such tracts as may from time to time be required or taken up for settlement, mining, lumbering or other purposes by Her said Government of the Dominion of Canada, or by any of the subjects thereof duly authorized therefor by the said Government.

It is further agreed between Her Majesty and Her said Indians, that such sections of the reserves above indicated as may at any time be required for public works or buildings, of what nature soever, may be appropriated for that purpose by Her Majesty's Government of the Dominion of Canada, due compensation being made for the value of any improvements thereon.

And further, that Her Majesty's Commissioners shall, as soon as possible after the execution of this treaty, cause to be taken an accurate census of all the Indians inhabiting the tract above described, distributing them in families, and shall, in every year ensuing the date hereof, at some period in each year, to be duly notified to the Indians, and at a place or places to be appointed for that purpose within the territory ceded, pay to each Indian person the sum of $5 per head yearly.

It is further agreed between Her Majesty and the said Indians, that the sum of $1,500.00 per annum shall be yearly and every year expended by Her Majesty in the purchase of ammunition, and twine for nets, for the use of the said Indians, in manner following, that is to say: In the reasonable discretion, as regards the distribution thereof among the Indians inhabiting the several reserves, or otherwise, included herein, of Her Majesty's Indian Agent having the supervision of this treaty.

It is further agreed between Her Majesty and the said Indians, that the following articles shall be supplied to any Band of the said Indians who are now cultivating the soil, or who shall hereafter commence to cultivate the land, that is to say: Four hoes for every family actually cultivating; also, two spades per family as aforesaid: one plough for every three families, as aforesaid; one harrow for every three families, as aforesaid; two scythes and one whetstone, and two hay forks and two reaping hooks, for every family as aforesaid, and also two axes; and also one cross-cut saw, one hand-saw, one pit-saw, the necessary files, one grindstone and one auger for each Band; and also for each Chief for the use of his Band, one chest of ordinary carpenter's tools; also, for each Band, enough of wheat, barley, potatoes and oats to plant the land actually broken up for cultivation by such Band; also for each Band four oxen, one bull and six cows; also, one boar and two sows, and one hand-mill when any Band shall raise sufficient grain therefor. All the aforesaid articles to be given once and for all for the encouragement of the practice of agriculture among the Indians.

It is further agreed between Her Majesty and the said Indians, that each Chief, duly recognized as such, shall receive an annual salary of twenty-five dollars per annum; and each subordinate officer, not exceeding four for each Band, shall receive fifteen dollars per annum; and each such Chief and subordinate officer, as aforesaid, shall also receive once every three years, a suitable suit of clothing, and each Chief shall receive, in recognition of the closing of the treaty, a suitable flag and medal, and also as soon as convenient, one horse, harness and waggon.

That in the event hereafter of the Indians comprised within this treaty being overtaken by any pestilence, or by a general famine, the Queen, on being satisfied and certified thereof by Her Indian Agent or Agents, will grant to the Indians assistance of such character and to such extent as Her Chief Superintendent of Indian Affairs shall deem necessary and sufficient to relieve the Indians from the calamity that shall have befallen them.

That during the next three years, after two or more of the reserves hereby agreed to be set apart to the Indians shall have been agreed upon and surveyed, there shall be granted to the Indians included under the Chiefs adhering to the treaty at Carlton, each spring, the sum of one thousand dollars, to be expended for them by Her

Majesty's Indian Agents, in the purchase of provisions for the use of such of the Band as are actually settled on the reserves and are engaged in cultivating the soil, to assist them in such cultivation.

That a medicine chest shall be kept at the house of each Indian Agent for the use and benefit of the Indians at the direction of such agent.

That with regard to the Indians included under the Chiefs adhering to the treaty at Fort Pitt, and to those under Chiefs within the treaty limits who may hereafter give their adhesion thereto (exclusively, however, of the Indians of the Carlton region), there shall, during three years, after two or more reserves shall have been agreed upon and surveyed be distributed each spring among the Bands cultivating the soil on such reserves, by Her Majesty's Chief Indian Agent for this treaty, in his discretion, a sum not exceeding one thousand dollars, in the purchase of provisions for the use of such members of the Band as are actually settled on the reserves and engaged in the cultivation of the soil, to assist and encourage them in such cultivation.

That in lieu of waggons, if they desire it and declare their option to that effect, there shall be given to each of the Chiefs adhering hereto at Fort Pitt or elsewhere hereafter (exclusively of those in the Carlton district), in recognition of this treaty, as soon as the same can be conveniently transported, two carts with iron bushings and tires.

And the undersigned Chiefs on their own behalf and on behalf of all other Indians inhabiting the tract within ceded, do hereby solemnly promise and engage to strictly observe this treaty, and also to conduct and behave themselves as good and loyal subjects of Her Majesty the Queen.

They promise and engage that they will in all respects obey and abide by the law, and they will maintain peace and good order between each other, and also between themselves and other tribes of Indians, and between themselves and others of Her Majesty's subjects, whether Indians or whites, now inhabiting or hereafter to inhabit any part of the said ceded tracts, and that they will not molest the person or property of any inhabitant of such ceded tracts, or the property of Her Majesty the Queen, or interfere with or trouble any person passing or travelling through the said tracts, or any part thereof, and that they will aid and assist the officers of Her Majesty in bringing to justice and punishment any Indian offending against the stipulations of this treaty, or infringing the laws in force in the country so ceded.

IN WITNESS WHEREOF, Her Majesty's said Commissioners and the said Indian Chiefs have hereunto subscribed and set their hands at or near Fort Carlton, on the days and year aforesaid, and near Fort Pitt on the day above aforesaid.

NOTES

1   Johnson, *Two Families*.
2   Quoted in Newman, *Caesars of the Wilderness*, 110.
3   Ibid., 113–14.
4   Quoted in MacAndrew and Edgerton, *Drunken Comportment*, 104.
5   Ibid., 102.
6   Quoted in O'Meara, *Last Portage*, 136.
7   Franklin, *Autobiography*, 67–68. Franklin began writing his autobiography in 1771. He continued it again in 1784 and did not write this passage until 1788.
8   As spoken by the Cree Council. Quoted in Morris, *Treaties of Canada*, 174.
9   Johnson, *Two Families*, 27.
10 Morris, *Treaties of Canada*, 185.
11 *The Queen v. Drybones* [1970] S.C.R. 282.
12 Irvine et al., "Northern Saskatchewan Health Indicators Report."
13 See, for example: McNamee and Offord, "Suicide Prevention," 143.
14 See, for example: Briasoulis et al., "Alcohol Consumption"; Fernández-Solà, "Cardiovascular Risks"; Klatsky and Gunderson, "Alcohol and Hypertension"; Patra et al., "Alcohol Consumption"; and Rehm et al., "Alcohol and Cardiovascular Disease."
15 See, for example: Brien et al., "Effect of Alcohol Consumption"; and Fekjaer, "Alcohol."
16 See, for example: Rehm et al., "Global Burden of Disease"; World Health Organization, *Global Status Report*; World Health Organization, "Alcohol. Fact Sheet"; Bagnardi et al., "Light Alcohol Drinking"; Lee and Hashibe, "Tobacco, Alcohol and Cancer"; Parry et al., "Alcohol Consumption"; Pelucchi et al., "Alcohol Consumption"; Baan et al., "Carcinogenicity of Alcoholic Beverages"; de Menezes et al., "Alcohol Consumption"; Islami et al., "Alcohol Drinking"; Li et al., "Alcohol Drinking"; Scoccianti et al., "Recent Evidence"; Singletary and Gapstur, "Alcohol and Breast Cancer"; and Turati et al., "Alcohol and Liver Cancer."
17 Public Health Agency of Canada, "Chief Public Health Officer's Report," 13. Global statistics are reported by Praud et

al. in "Cancer Incidence and Mortality," with the following percentages of alcohol-attributable cancer cases for these specific cancers: oral-throat (36.7 per cent), esophagus (44.7 per cent), colon-rectum (9.2 per cent), liver (12.9 per cent), gallbladder (15.6 per cent), pancreas (3.5 per cent), larynx (26.1 per cent), and breast (7.3 per cent).

18   International Agency for Research on Cancer, "Monographs."

19   Public Health Agency of Canada, "Chief Public Health Officer's Report," 3.

20   Rehm et al., "Global Burden of Disease."

21   See World Health Organization, *Global Status Report*; World Health Organization, "Alcohol. Fact Sheet"; and World Health Organization, "Top 10 Causes of Death."

22   Royal Commission on Aboriginal Peoples, *Report*, 144.

23   Ibid.

24   Ibid., 147.

25   See, for example: Macdonald, "Canada's Prisons"; and Jackson, "Locking up Natives."

26   *R. v. Gladue*, [1999] 1 S.C.R. 688, par. 67.

27   McGillivray, *Journal*, 47.

28   Kline et al., "Increased Risk of Alcohol Dependency."

29   See, for example: Walsh et al., "Trauma Exposure"; and Simpson et al., "Drinking Motives."

30   Truth and Reconciliation Commission of Canada, *Final Report*.

31   See Mercredi and Turpel (Lafond), *In the Rapids*.

32   "Rarely have we seen a person fail who has thoroughly followed our path. Those that do not recover are people who cannot or will not completely give themselves to this simple program, usually men and women who are constitutionally incapable of being honest with themselves": Bill W., *Alcoholics Anonymous*, 58. (This book is generally known as the *Big Book* because of the thickness of the paper used in the first edition in 1939.)

33   See, for example: Dodes and Dodes, *Sober Truth;* and Thatcher, *Fighting Firewater Fictions*.

34   Ogborne and Glaser, "Evaluating Alcoholics Anonymous."

35   Baker, *Introduction to English Legal History*.

36   See, for example: Unger and Smolin, *Singular Universe*; and Gleiser, *Island of Knowledge*.

37   Hawking, *Brief History of Time*, 7–9.

38 Public Health Agency of Canada, "Chief Public Health Officer's Report," 34.

39 See, for example: McCarthy et al., "Acute Alcohol Effects"; Townshend et al., "Binge Drinking"; and Aertgeerts and Buntinx, "Relation between Alcohol Abuse."

40 http://www.finance.gov.sk.ca/taxes/lct/.

41 http://www.finance.gov.sk.ca/PlanningandReporting/2014-15/JusticePlan1415.pdf, 29.

42 Personal conversation with Assistant Commissioner Russ Mirasty, commanding officer of F Division of the RCMP. Conversation repeated 27 February 2016.

43 http://www.finance.gov.sk.ca/PlanningandReporting/2014-15/HealthPlan1415-print.pdf.

44 I continue to participate in the commercial fishery on a very small scale. It seems part of my heritage. My father and grandfather were commercial fishers.

45 See Rehm et al., "Costs of Substance Abuse."

46 See McLeod, "Coming Home Through Stories."

47 "Our bondage to society is not so much established by conquest as by collusion. Sometimes, indeed, we are crushed into submission. Much more frequently we are entrapped by our own social nature. The walls of our imprisonment were there before we appeared on the scene, but they are ever rebuilt by ourselves. We are betrayed into captivity with our own cooperation": Berger, *Invitation to Sociology*, 121.

48 See Romo, "'Above the Influence.'"

49 See Thatcher, *Fighting Firewater Fictions*, 73–95.

50 "Much in our modern ideas about society represents the relentless development of the principle contained in Vico's [Giambattista] statement that man can understand the social world because he made it": Unger, *Social Theory*, 84. Vico Giambattista (1668-1744) is recognized as one of the great Enlightenment thinkers.

51 See Manning et al., "Wheeler's Delayed-Choice Gedanken Experiment."

52 Albert Einstein (1879–1955) was a German theoretical physicist.

53 See, for example: Tegmark, *Our Mathematical Universe*, 95–119; and Penrose, *Road to Reality*, 752.

54 Kaku, *Future of the Mind*, 36.

55 Gorshkov, *Physical and Biological Bases*.

NOTES

56   John 1:1.

57   Tegmark, *Our Mathematical Universe*, 10–11.

58   Indian Act. R.S., c. I-6, s. 85.1.

59   See Chandler and Lalonde, "Cultural Continuity."

60   See Roth, *American Homicide*.

61   Orwell, *Nineteen Eighty-Four*, 267.

62   Royal Commission on Aboriginal Peoples, *Report*, 159.

63   First Nations Information Governance Centre, *National Report*, 34.

64   From Ron Capps's presentation at the South Dakota Festival of Books, September 2015.

GLOSSARY OF CREE WORDS

-apoy (suffix)............................ liquid
Cihcipistikwân .... Wîsahkicâhk's mother
iskotîw .... fire
iskotîwapoy............................. alcohol (literally trans-
                                     lates as "fire" + "water")
kayâs..................................... a long time ago, or maybe
                                     "once upon a time"
ketayayak............................... Elders
kiciwamanawak .... our cousins (white
                                     settler Canadians)
kitaskinâw.............................. our land
mahikan .... wolf
mikisîw .... bald eagle
mithosin .... beautiful
maskwa.................................. bear
kakithaw niwâhkomakanak ... all my relatives
nîhithaw .... Cree
nimisak .... my older sisters
nisimisak................................ my younger siblings
nistîsak .... my older brothers
niyâk...................................... for the future
paskwa mostos....................... bison
tanisi...................................... hello
wetiko .... cannibal monster
Wîsahkicâhk............................. trickster

SOURCES AND FURTHER READING

BOOKS AND ARTICLES

Anderson, Karen. *Chain Her by One Foot: The Subjugation of Native Women in Seventeenth-Century New France*. New York: Routledge, 1991.

Angus, Patricia Monture. *Thunder in My Soul: A Mohawk Woman Speaks*. Halifax: Fernwood Publishing, 1995.

Baker, John H. *An Introduction to English Legal History*. 3rd ed. London: Butterworth and Co., 1990.

Berger, Peter L. *Invitation to Sociology: A Humanistic Perspective*. New York: Doubleday, 1963.

Berger, Thomas. *Northern Frontier Northern Homeland: The Report of the Mackenzie Valley Pipeline Inquiry*. Vancouver: Douglas and McIntyre Ltd., 1977.

Bill W. *Alcoholics Anonymous: The Story of How Many Thousands of Men and Women Have Recovered from Alcoholism*. New York: Alcoholics Anonymous World Services, Inc.

Campbell, Joseph. *The Hero with a Thousand Faces*. 2nd ed. Princeton: Princeton University Press, 1968.

Chandler, Michael J., and Christopher E. Lalonde. "Cultural Continuity as a Moderator of Suicide Risk among Canada's First Nations." In *Healing Traditions: The Mental Health of Aboriginal Peoples in Canada*, edited by Laurence J. Kirmayer and Gail Guthrie Valaskakis, 221–48. Vancouver: University of British Columbia Press, 2009.

Churchill, Ward. *Struggle for the Land: Native North American Resistance to Genocide, Ecocide and Colonization*. Winnipeg: Arbeiter Ring Publishing, 1999.

Gosse, Richard, James Youngblood Henderson, and Roger Carter, eds. *Continuing Poundmaker and Riel's Quest: Presentations Made at a Conference on Aboriginal Peoples and Justice*. Saskatoon: Purich Publishing, 1994.

Diamond, Jared. *Guns, Germs, and Steel: The Fates of Human Societies*. New York: W.W. Norton and Company, 1999.

Dodes, Lance, and Zachary Dodes. *The Sober Truth: Debunking the Bad Science Behind 12-Step Programs and the Rehab Industry*. Boston: Beacon Press, 2014.

Elk, Black. *The Sacred Pipe, Black Elk's Account of the Seven Rites of the Oglala Sioux*. Recorded and edited by Joseph Epes Brown. Norman: University of Oklahoma Press, 1953.

First Nations Information Governance Centre. *National Report on Adults, Youth and Children Living in First Nations Communities*. First Nations Regional Health Survey (RHS) Phase 2 (2008/10). Ottawa: The First Nations Information Governance Centre, 2012.

Franklin, Benjamin. *The Autobiography of Benjamin Franklin*. Cambridge, MA: Houghton, Mifflin and Company/The Riverside Press, 1888.

Gleiser, Marcelo. *The Island of Knowledge: The Limits of Science and the Search for Meaning*. New York: Basic Books, 2014.

Gorshkov, Victor G. *Physical and Biological Bases of Life Stability: Man, Biota, Environment*. Berlin, Heidelberg: Springer-Verlag, 1995.

Halfe, Sky Dancer Louise. *The Crooked Good*. Regina: Coteau Books, 2007.

Hawking, Stephen. *A Brief History of Time*. New York: Bantam Books, 1996.

Hutchison, George, and Dick Wallace. *Grassy Narrows*. Toronto: Van Nostrand-Reinhold, 1977.

Indian Act. *Revised Statutes of Canada*. 1985, c. I-6, s. 85. http://laws-lois.justice.gc.ca/eng/acts/i-5/fulltext.html.

Jackson, Michael. "Locking up Natives in Canada: A Report of the Committee of the Canadian Bar Association on Imprisonment and Release." *University of British Columbia Law Review* 23 (1989): 215–300.

Johnson, Harold. *Two Families: Treaties and Government*. Saskatoon: Purich Publishing, 2007.

Kaku, Michio. *The Future of the Mind: The Scientific Quest to Understand, Enhance and Empower the Mind*. New York: Doubleday Publishing, 2014.

Kinew, Wab. *The Reason You Walk: A Memoir*. Toronto: Penguin Random House Canada, 2015.

King, Thomas. *The Truth about Stories: A Native Narrative*. Toronto: House of Anansi Press, 2003.

Lindberg, Tracey. *Birdie*. Toronto: HarperCollins Canada, 2015.

MacAndrew, Craig, and Robert B. Edgerton. *Drunken Comportment: A Social Explanation*. Chicago: Aldine, 1969.

Macdonald, Nancy. "Canada's Prisons Are the 'New Residential Schools.'" *Maclean's,* 18 February 2016. http://www.macleans.ca/news/canada/canadas-prisons-are-the-new-residential-schools/.

Mails, Thomas E. *Fools Crow: Wisdom and Power.* Tulsa: Council Oaks Books, 1991.

Man, Ed McGaa Eagle. *Mother Earth Spirituality: Native American Paths to Healing Ourselves and Our World.* New York: HarperCollins, 1990.

Manning, A. G., R. I. Khakimov, R. G. Dall, and A. G. Truscott. "Wheeler's Delayed-Choice Gedanken Experiment with a Single Atom." *Nature Physics* 11 (2015): 539–42.

Martins, Tony. *The Spirit Weeps: Characteristics and Dynamics of Incest and Child Sex Abuse.* Edmonton: Nechi Institute, 1988.

McAdam, Sylvia (Saysewahum). *Nationhood Interrupted: Revitalizing Nehiyaw Legal Systems.* Saskatoon: Purich Publishing, 2015.

McGillivray, Duncan. *The Journal of Duncan McGillivray of the North West Company at Fort George on the Saskatchewan, 1794-5.* Edited by Arthur S. Morton. Toronto: Macmillan, 1929.

McLeod, Neal. "Coming Home Through Stories." In *(Ad)dressing Our Words: Aboriginal Perspectives on Aboriginal Literatures,* edited by Armand Garnet Ruffo, 17–36. Penticton: Theytus Books, 2001.

McNamee, Jane, and D. R. Offord. "Suicide Prevention: A Canadian Perspective." In *Preventing Disease: Beyond the Rhetoric,* edited by Richard B. Goldbloom and Robert S. Lawrence, 137–48. New York: Springer-Verlag, 1990.

Mercredi, Ovide, and Mary Ellen Turpel [Lafond]. *In the Rapids: Navigating the Future of First Nations.* Toronto: Penguin Books, 1993.

Morris, Alexander. *The Treaties of Canada with the Indians of Manitoba and the Northwest Territories including the Negotiations on which they were based, and other information relating thereto.* Saskatoon: Fifth House, 1991.

Newman, Peter C. *Caesars of the Wilderness.* Toronto: Penguin Books, 1987.

O'Meara, Walter. *The Last Portage.* Boston: Houghton Mifflin, 1962.

Ogborne, Alan C., and Frederick B. Glaser. "Evaluating Alcoholics Anonymous." In *Alcoholism and Substance Abuse: Strategies for Clinical Intervention,* edited by Thomas E. Bratter and Gary G. Forrest, 176–92. New York: The Free Press, 1985.

Orwell, George. *Nineteen Eighty-Four*. New York: Penguin Signet Classic Paperback, 1961.

Penrose, Roger. *The Road to Reality: A Complete Guide to the Laws of the Universe*. New York: Vintage Books, 2004.

Ray, Arthur J., Jim Miller, and Frank Tough. *Bounty and Benevolence: A History of Saskatchewan Treaties*. Montreal and Kingston: McGill-Queen's University Press, 2000.

Roth, Randolph. *American Homicide*. Cambridge: Harvard University Press, 2009.

Royal Commission on Aboriginal Peoples. *Report*. Volume 3: *Gathering Strength*. Ottawa: The Commission, 1996. https://qspace. library.queensu.ca/bitstream/1974/6874/3/RRCAP3_combined.pdf.

Saskatchewan, Government of. *Keep Saskatchewan Strong*. http:// www.finance.gov.sk.ca/taxes/lct/.

———. *Ministry of Health and Healthcare System: Plan for 2014-15*. http://www.finance.gov.sk.ca/PlanningandReporting/2014-15/HealthPlan1415-print.pdf.

———. *Ministry of Justice: Plan for 2014-15*. http://www.finance.gov. sk.ca/PlanningandReporting/2014-15/JusticePlan1415.pdf.

Settee, Priscilla. *The Strength of Women: Âhkamêyimowak*. Regina: Coteau Books, 2011.

Slotkin, Richard. *Regeneration Through Violence: The Mythology of the American Frontier, 1600-1860*. Middletown: Wesleyan University Press, 1973.

Tegmark, Max. *Our Mathematical Universe: My Quest for the Ultimate Nature of Reality*. New York: Alfred A. Knopf, 2014.

Thatcher, Richard W. *Fighting Firewater Fictions: Moving Beyond the Disease Model of Alcoholism in First Nations*. Toronto: University of Toronto Press, 2004.

Thatcher, Richard W., and Fred E. Knowles, Jr. *The Circle Fellowship: A Members' Guide to Organizing and Participating in a Sobriety Support Group in Native American, First Nations, Inuit and Metis Communities*. Vernon, BC: Charlton Publishing, 2015.

Truth and Reconciliation Commission of Canada. *Final Report*. 2015. http://www.trc.ca/websites/trcinstitution/index.php?p=890.

Unger, Roberto Mangabeira. *Social Theory: Its Situation and Its Task, A Critical Introduction to Politics, A Work in Constructive Theory*. Cambridge: Cambridge University Press, 1987.

Unger, Roberto Mangabeira, and Lee Smolin. *The Singular Universe and the Reality of Time: A Proposal in Natural Philosophy*. Cambridge: Cambridge University Press, 2015.

Vandergoot, Mary E. *Justice for Young Offenders: Their Needs, Our Responses*. Saskatoon: Purich Publishing, 2006.

Van Camp, Richard. *The Lesser Blessed*. Vancouver: Douglas and McIntyre, 2012.

Williams, Robert A., Jr. *The American Indian in Western Legal Thought: The Discourses of Conquest*. New York: Oxford University Press, 1990.

COURT CASES

R. v. Gladue, [1999] 1 S.C.R. 688. http://www.canlii.org/en/ca/scc/doc/1999/1999canlii679/1999canlii679.html

The Queen v. Drybones [1970] S.C.R. 282. https://scc-csc.lexum.com/scc-csc/scc-csc/en/item/2722/index.do

STUDIES AND REPORTS ON ALCOHOL AND HEALTH

Aertgeerts, B., and Buntinx F. "The Relation between Alcohol Abuse or Dependence and Academic Performance in First-Year College Students." *The Journal of Adolescent Health* 31, no. 3 (2002): 223–25.

Baan, R., K. Straif, Y. Grosse, B. Secretan, F. El Ghissassi, V. Bouvard, A. Altieri, and V. Cogliano. "Carcinogenicity of Alcoholic Beverages." *Lancet Oncology* 8, no. 4 (2007): 292–93.

Bagnardi, V., M. Rota, E. Botteri, I. Tramacere, F. Islami, V. Fedirko, L. Scotti, M. Jenab, F. Turati, E. Pasquali, C. Pelucchi, R. Bellocco, E. Negri, G. Corrao, J. Rehm, P. Boffetta, and C. La Vecchia. "Light Alcohol Drinking and Cancer: A Meta-analysis." *Annals of Oncology* 24, no.2 (2013): 301–8.

Briasoulis, A., V. Agarwal, and F. H. Messerli. "Alcohol Consumption and the Risk of Hypertension in Men and Women: A Systematic Review and Meta-analysis." *Journal of Clinical Hypertension* 14, no. 11 (2012): 792–98.

Brien, S. E., P. E. Ronksley, B. J. Turner, K. J. Mukamal, and W. A. Ghali. "Effect of Alcohol Consumption on Biological Markers Associated with Risk of Coronary Heart Disease: Systemic Review and Meta Analysis of Interventional Studies." *BMJ* 342 (2011): d636.

de Menezes, R. F., A. Bergmann, and L. C. Thuler. "Alcohol Consumption and Risk of Cancer: A Systematic Literature Review." *Asian Pacific Journal of Cancer Prevention* 14, no. 9 (2013): 4965–72. Fekjaer, H. O. "Alcohol—A Universal Preventive Agent? A Critical Analysis." *Addiction* 108, no. 12 (2013): 2051–57.

Fernández-Solà, J. "Cardiovascular Risks and Benefits of Moderate and Heavy Alcohol Consumption." *Nature Reviews Cardiology* (2015). http://www.nature.com/nrcardio/journal/v12/n10/full/nrcardio.2015.91.html

International Agency for Research on Cancer. "Monographs on the Evaluation of Carcinogenic Risks to Humans" (28 February 2016). http://monographs.iarc.fr/ENG/Classification.

Irvine, J., B. Quinn, and D. Stockdale. "Northern Saskatchewan Health Indicators Report 2011." Athabasca Health Authority and Keewatin Yatthé and Mamawetan Churchill River Regional Health Authorities. Population Health Unit, La Ronge, SK, 2011.

Islami, F., I. Tramacere, M. Rota, V. Bagnardi, V. Fedirko, L. Scotti, W. Garavello, M. Jenab, G. Corrao, K. Straif, E. Negri, P. Boffetta, and C. La Vecchia. "Alcohol Drinking and Laryngeal Cancer: Overall and Dose-Risk Relation—A Systematic Review and Meta-analysis." *Oral Oncology* 46, no. 11 (2010): 802–10.

Klatsky, A. L., and E. Gunderson. "Alcohol and Hypertension: A Review." *Journal of the American Society of Hypertension* 2, no. 5 (2008): 307–17.

Kline, A., M. D. Weiner, D. S. Ciccone, A. Interian, L. St Hill, and M. Losonczy. "Increased Risk of Alcohol Dependency in a Cohort of National Guard Troops with PTSD: A Longitudinal Study." *Journal of Psychiatric Research* 50 (2014): 18–25.

Lee, Y. C., and M. Hashibe. "Tobacco, Alcohol and Cancer in Low and High Income Countries." *Annals of Global Health* 80, no. 5 (2014): 378–83.

Li, Y., Y. Mao, Y. Zhang, S. Cai, G. Chen, Y. Ding, J. Guo, K. Chen, and M. Jin. "Alcohol Drinking and Upper Aerodigestive Tract Cancer Mortality: A Systematic Review and Meta-analysis." *Oral Oncology* 50, no. 4 (2014): 269–75.

McCarthy, D. M., M. E. Niculete, H. R. Treloar, D. H. Morris, and B. D. Bartholow. "Acute Alcohol Effects on Impulsivity: Associations with Drinking and Drinking Behavior." *Addiction* 107, no. 2 (2012): 2109–14.

Parry, C. D., J. Patra, and J. Rehm. "Alcohol Consumption and Non-communicable Diseases: Epidemiology and Policy Implications." *Addiction* 106, no. 10 (2011): 1718–24.

Patra, J., B. Taylor, H. Irving, M. Roerecke, D. Baliunas, S. Mohapatra, and J. Rehm. "Alcohol Consumption and the Risk of Morbidity and Mortality for Different Stroke Types—A Systematic Review and Meta-analysis." *BMC Public Health* 10 (2010): 258.

Pelucchi, C., I. Tramacere, P. Boffetta, E. Negri, and C. La Vecchia. "Alcohol Consumption and Cancer Risk." *Nutrition and Cancer* 63, no. 7 (2011): 983–90.

Praud, D., M. Rota, J. Rehm, K. Shield, W. Zatoński, M. Hashibe, C. La Vecchia, and P. Boffetta. "Cancer Incidence and Mortality Attributable to Alcohol Consumption." *International Journal of Cancer* 138 (2016): 1380–87.

Public Health Agency of Canada. "The Chief Public Health Officer's Report on the State of Public Health in Canada, 2015: Alcohol Consumption in Canada." http://healthycanadians.gc.ca/publications/department-ministere/state-public-health-alcohol-2015-etat-sante-publique-alcool/index-eng.php.

Rehm, J., D. Ballunas, S. Brochu, B. Fischer, W. Gnam, J. Patra, S. Popova, A. Sarnocinska-Hart, and B. Taylor. "The Costs of Substance Abuse in Canada 2002." Canadian Centre on Substance Abuse, 2006. http://www.ccsa.ca/Resource%20Library/ccsa-011332-2006.pdf.

Rehm, J., C. Mathers, S. Popova, M. Thavorncharoensap, Y. Teerawattananon, and J. Patra. "Global Burden of Disease and Injury and Economic Cost Attributable to Alcohol Use and Alcohol-Use Disorders." *Lancet* 373, no. 9682 (2009): 2223–33.

Rehm, J., C. T. Sempos, and M. Trevisan. "Alcohol and Cardiovascular Disease—More than One Paradox to Consider. Average Volume of Alcohol Consumption, Patterns of Drinking and Risk of Coronary Heart Disease—A Review." *Journal of Cardiovascular Risk* 10, no. 1 (2003): 15–20.

Rehm, J., B. Taylor, and R. Room. "Global Burden of Disease from Alcohol, Illicit Drugs and Tobacco." *Drug and Alcohol Review* 25, no. 6 (2006): 503–13.

Romo, L. K. "'Above the Influence': How College Students Communicate about the Healthy Deviance of Alcohol Abstinence." *Health Communication* 27, no. 7 (2012): 672–81.

Scoccianti, C., K. Straif, and I. Romieu. "Recent Evidence on Alcohol and Cancer Epidemiology." *Future Oncology* 9, no. 9 (2013): 1315–22.

Seitz, H. K., C. Pelucchi, V. Bagnardi, and C. La Vecchia. "Epidemiology and Pathophysiology of Alcohol and Breast Cancer: Update 2012." *Alcohol and Alcoholism* 47, no. 3 (2012): 204–12.

Simpson, T. L., C. A. Stappenbeck, J. A. Luterek, K. Lehavot, and D. L. Kaysen. "Drinking Motives Moderate Daily Relationships between PTSD Symptoms and Alcohol Use." *Journal of Abnormal Psychology* 123, no. 1 (2014): 237–47.

Singletary, K. W., and S. M. Gapstur. "Alcohol and Breast Cancer: Review of Epidemiologic and Experimental Evidence and Potential Mechanisms." *Journal of the American Medical Association* 286, no. 17 (2001): 2143–51.

Townshend, J. M., N. Kambouropoulos, A. Griffin, F. J. Hunt, and R. M. Milani. "Binge Drinking, Reflection Impulsivity, and Unplanned Sexual Behavior: Impaired Decision-Making in Young Social Drinkers." *Alcoholism: Clinical and Experimental Research* 38, no. 4 (2014): 1143–50.

Turati, F., C. Galeone, M. Rota, C. Pelucchi, E. Negri, V. Bagnardi, G. Corrao, P. Boffetta, and C. La Vecchia. "Alcohol and Liver Cancer: A Systematic Review and Meta-analysis of Prospective Studies." *Annals of Oncology* 25, no. 8 (2014): 1526–35.

Walsh, K., J. C. Elliott, D. Shmulewitz, E. Aharonovich, R. Strous, A. Frisch, A. Weizman, B. Spivak, B. F. Grant, and D. Hasin. "Trauma Exposure, Post-traumatic Stress Disorder and Risk for Alcohol, Nicotine, and Marijuana Dependence in Israel." *Comprehensive Psychiatry* 55, no. 3 (2014): 621–30.

World Health Organization. "Alcohol. Fact sheet" (January 2015). http://www.who.int/mediacentre/factsheets/fs349/en/.

———. *Global Status Report on Alcohol and Health*. Switzerland: WHO Press, 2014.

———. "The Top 10 Causes of Death. Fact Sheet" (May 2014). http://www.who.int/mediacentre/factsheets/fs310/en/.

INDEX

ABOUT THE AUTHOR

Harold Johnson is a member of the Montreal Lake Cree Nation. After a stint in the Canadian Navy, he has been a logger, miner, trapper, fisher, mechanic, firefighter, heavy equipment operator, smelter worker, tree planter, trade unionist, educator, and writer. He left mining to go to the University of Saskatchewan, where he earned a bachelor's degree in law, and to Harvard University, where he completed a master's degree in law. After some time as in-house counsel for a trade union and as a researcher and in private practice, Harold is now a senior Crown prosecutor in La Ronge, Saskatchewan. He and his wife, Joan, live off-grid on his family trapline, where they trap and fish and maintain contact with the natural world. Harold has published five works of fiction. His previous non-fiction work, *Two Families: Treaties and Government*, examined Canadian constitutionalism from a Cree law perspective.

Printed in the USA
CPSIA information can be obtained
at www.ICGtesting.com
JSHW020734030324
58418JS00001B/33